MIND WARS

MIND WARS:
The True Story of Government Research into the Military Potential of Psychic Weapons

RONALD M. McRAE

ST. MARTIN'S PRESS · NEW YORK

To my mother, Margaret Niland McRae
(the royalty checks I dedicate to my father)

Easter Lilies

White,
Holy and Madonna-like
Lilies in a row;
Green hills
Kissed with snow.
Margaret Niland, 1934

MIND WARS. Copyright © 1984 by Ronald M. McRae. All rights reserved. Printed in the United States of America. No part of this book may be used or reproduced in any manner whatsoever without written permission except in the case of brief quotations embodied in critical articles or reviews. For information, address St. Martin's Press, 175 Fifth Avenue, New York, N.Y. 10010.

Design by Nancy Dale Muldoon

Library of Congress Cataloging in Publication Data

McRae, Ronald M.
  Mind wars.

  1. Psychical research—Military aspects. I. Title.
BF1045.M55M34 1984   133.8'024355   83-21241
ISBN 0-312-65231-3

First Edition
10 9 8 7 6 5 4 3 2 1

CONTENTS

A NOTE FROM THE AUTHOR ON JOURNALISTS AND SCIENTISTS

I AM not a scientist. I do read *Scientific American* and can understand about half of it.

Except for those who write for publications like *Scientific American* and *Discover,* few journalists even attempt to keep up with what's news in science. Few could. I fear that the half of *Scientific American* that I do comprehend will shrink, page by page, as newer theories and more exotic formulas expand the horizons of current knowledge.

Unfortunately, today journalists often find they need to understand those exotic formulas. Recently, Dale Van Atta, a Jack Anderson associate, obtained top secret plans to deploy the neutron bomb with U.S. troops in Korea—just the sort of coup that has made Jack Anderson's column famous. Twenty years ago, the document would have been the story. Today, even that relatively nontechnical paper—it was written for professional soldiers, not physicists—needed some interpretation. Just what does

$$\text{Yield} = 1.1 \text{ KT} + .8 \text{ ER}$$

mean?,* Dale wondered.

No matter what the field, science often determines the news.

---

*The formula expresses the explosive power (Yield) of the neutron bomb as the sum of blast (KT) and radiation (ER).

The president's economists promise "high tech" will wipe out unemployment. Buck Rogers technology dominates medical news: artificial hearts, organ transplants, gene splicing. Even a reporter on the high school beat might find his biggest story is computers in the classroom.

I personally believe reporters must specialize. Whether his beat is the economy, medicine, or the school board, a reporter must become conversant enough with the new technologies to interpret the words of the researchers for the now-bewildered public.

Of course, reporters need the active cooperation of the scientists, and that cooperation is often not forthcoming. Scientists don't, as a rule, make good press agents. They speculate more cautiously than the press, which depends more on rumor and anonymous sources than carefully documented columns and rows of figures.

Fortunately, some scientists will cooperate, and I have been most fortunate in finding one such man. I have asked Marcello Truzzi, a distinguished sociologist and a leading authority on the so-called deviant sciences, to comment on the remarkable and sometimes bizarre new technologies I have uncovered in writing this book.

Truzzi is a rarity in the Byzantine field of psychic research, a field where conspiracy seems as common as experimentation. Truzzi is trusted. Both the parapsychologists and the skeptics universally concede Marcello Truzzi is objective and unbiased.

The responsibility for the accuracy of the facts I allege in this book is wholly my own. Professor Truzzi kindly corrected the many technical errors in my original draft, but I, and I alone, waded through that "sea of conjectures, rumors, and confusion" that, as Professor Truzzi notes in his foreword, baffles even those who work in the field. My conclusions, right or wrong, are mine.

FOREWORD BY MARCELLO TRUZZI

Much that Ron McRae reveals to us in *Mind Wars* will strike some readers as preposterous and others as incredible but true. To some degree, both will be right. Those of us who have been attempting to monitor government interest in and involvement with parapsychology are faced with a Byzantine labyrinth of both information and *disinformation*, intentional misinformation put out by agencies to mislead and hide the truth. Only a few things seem certain. We know that the governments of the United States and the Soviet Union (and more recently the Chinese government) have shown serious interest in the claims of parapsychology and have sponsored research in the area. We know that much of this work has been conducted clandestinely and in conjunction with military and intelligence agencies. And we also know that there has been interest in this work expressed by some officials at the highest levels of government, including past presidents of the United States. But beyond this, there is mainly a sea of conjectures, rumors, and confusion. Most scientists, including parapsychologists, know little of these matters. Unearthing details takes the skills of an investigative reporter, and Ron McRae has dug up some quite remarkable information, much of which will surprise and shock even those who work in the field.

Those familiar with the history of clandestine operations during the Second World War are aware of the many both brilliant and outlandish intelligence ploys engaged in by our government.

Some of these involved "occult" areas. For example, the British used an astrologer to predict the sort of advice a German astrologer was reputedly giving Hitler. Since President Reagan has occasionally been reported to have a serious interest in astrology (denied by the White House), it seems likely that the Soviets have similarly sought to anticipate advice that might be given him by hiring their own astrologer. Such involvement by governments in arcane matters may be purely a practical matter and may have no deeper meaning. There are some who cynically believe that all of the U.S. government involvement with psi research is simply disinformation, misleading propaganda to make the Communists waste time and resources on such projects of their own. But there are also those at the other extreme who proclaim that the Soviets are far ahead of the West in the race for "inner space," and that these efforts constitute a clear and present danger to the vital security and military might of this country. As with most things, the truth probably lies somewhere in the middle.

As we read the documents available to us, especially those still largely censored documents available via the Freedom of Information Act, and locate the occasional news stories buried in the back pages of the press, it is often impossible to conclude if we are dealing with geniuses or madmen. For example, one scheme disclosed by Ron McRae proposed that we might be able to meet a nuclear-armed missile with a new psychotronic device that could cast the threatening weapon one hundred years into our future, at which time—when the rest of our technology had advanced to a level that might enable us to disarm it—we could deal with it properly (or presumably send it forward in time again and again until we could disarm it). Is such a science-fiction like scheme brilliant or insane? How do we judge a wild idea like this without adequate knowledge about the alleged psychotronic device and its real capabilities (if any)?

To most skeptics, all this may sound like madness, the replacement of reason with pseudoscience or Buck Rogers mythology.

But closer examination reveals a greater complexity. Scientists normally acknowledge two different kinds of possible errors that need to be avoided. The first kind, called a "Type I error" by statisticians, occurs when you mistakenly think something special is happening when in fact nothing beyond normal chance happenings is taking place. For example, if you thought taking a new pill was curing a symptom but actually the pill was doing nothing special, the symptom merely went away by itself, you'd be committing a Type I error. The second type of mistake, called a "Type II error," occurs when you mistakenly decide that nothing special is happening when in fact something special is taking place. If you conclude that the pill made no difference to the remedy when it actually had an effect, that would be making a Type II error.

Typically, we are especially concerned about not making a Type II error when there is special importance attached to a claimed effect.

Most scientists—including parapsychologists—admit that the evidence for psi remains scientifically unconvincing. The probability that real clairvoyance or precognition or psychokinesis actually exists is low. But if even one such claim turned out to be true, it could be of tremendous importance to the state of our national security. On purely scientific grounds, we might choose to ignore parapsychology until it gained greater acceptance among other scientists now skeptical and even hostile to its claims. But we are not dealing with purely scientific grounds. Our government has a responsibility to achieve security and military parity, if not superiority, in relation to our potential enemies. Thus, even if the probabilities for psi research producing anything practical are small, it would be negligence for our guardians in government to ignore such matters, especially when others are pursuing such avenues. Long shots have paid off in the past. Atomic energy was once a "wild idea." What if our enemies got success first?

Given all this, and given the astronomical budget being spent on conventional weapons, is it not reasonable to spend a modest amount on such long shots? Perhaps what is mainly happening is that the government is simply hedging its bets. But, as Ron McRae has uncovered, there also seem to be strong enthusiasts within the military who believe in and actively promote psi research. These proponents seem to envision applied parapsychology and psychotronic weaponry as part of our more immediate technology of the future. Such advocates talk of things like "psychic assassins" and fantastic new techniques for clairvoyant espionage. Are these "New Age" loonies who have got into responsible government positions, or do they know about secret breakthroughs to which the rest of us are not yet privy? It is simply impossible for those of us outside of security-protected channels to really know. Rumors within psi research circles abound. Some have put forward incredible conspiracy theories that link everything from the Soviet KGB and our own CIA with new religious movements and even unidentified flying objects. Others complain about what they perceive as an almost complete absence of any serious government interest in parapsychology. Some complain that the government is wasting money on pseudoscience. Others complain that we have probably already been overtaken by the Russians' breakthroughs. This book does not and cannot give us all the answers to such matters, but McRae has done a remarkable job in bringing to light much that has until now been in darkness. He has given us enough pieces of the puzzle so that we can now at least see some of the areas filled in enough to make a preliminary assessment and recognize that government psi efforts have been grossly publicly underestimated.

Parapsychologists have long recognized that there are three routes that might lead to the acceptance of psi. The first might come from an experiment that could produce psi upon demand, especially when conducted by skeptics. Although such an experiment does not exist, substantial progress seems to have been made, since parapsychologists today claim positive replication rates of over 50 percent for certain techniques, such as those used in remote viewing and in the Ganzfeld studies.* A second route toward mainstream science's acceptance of psi might come from an acceptable theory hospitable to psi phenomena. Again, progress exists since some ideas in the newer quantum physics might make permissible some phenomena (like going backward in time) previously considered impossible. The third route toward acceptance of psi might simply consist of finding a practical application that "works" whether or not it is completely reliable or fully understood. It is this route that apparently is being followed by government proponents of psi. Decision makers seem to be convinced that psi efforts can be "successful" in some potentially practical way. It doesn't have to completely make sense if you are convinced it "works."

On the surface, such a pragmatic approach may seem sensible. After all, if a psychic spy can get accurate information, why not use him/her? The trouble is that once such applications are enmeshed in secrecy (in the name of national security), accurate evaluation may become impossible. Those doing the work on such projects may have a vested interest in them, and the clandestine project can avoid outside criticism. When normally public science is conducted privately, the normal self-correcting mechanisms, the checks and balances provided by skeptics, may be largely eliminated. This could result in a case of the inmates running the asylum. That is why investigative journalism such as that by Ron McRae may prove important. In a democratic society, the public must retain some control over science done in the name of the state. Investigative reportage is a partial reply to the old question of who will guard us against our guardians. If government psi research is actually pseudoscience (and is not intended as disinformation), taxpayer money is being wasted. But if psi research is

---

*Ganzfeld studies are experiments in which the subject is shielded from unwanted sensory influences, sometimes by being placed blindfolded in a soundproof room.

valid, these incredible breakthroughs could end up being used not so much for our protection but as new and terrible tools for invasion of privacy and increased domestic control. Either way, these efforts have important consequences for all of us, and we have a right to know more than we do. Where there is smoke, there may be no fire, there may only be smoke (as physicist and critic of parapsychology John Wheeler recently reminded us); but Ron McRae has found an unusually large quantity of smoke, and fire or not, it may behoove us all to learn more about its origins.

—Marcello Truzzi, Ph.D.
Director, Center for Scientific
Anomalies Research

Professor Truzzi is Director of the Center for Scientific Anomalies Research (CSAR) in Ann Arbor, Michigan. The orientation of the Center is exclusively scientific. The Center places the burden of proof on the claimant, and recognizes that extraordinary claims demand commensurately extraordinary proof. But the one hundred plus scientists associated with the center and consultants do listen.

"We recognize that scientific anomalies, where valid, may be instruments and driving forces for the growth of scientific theory," says Truzzi, "History clearly demonstrates that tomorrow's science is likely to contain surprises, and tomorrow's theories are likely to explain some—but not all—of what are today viewed as controversial anomalies."

CSAR is currently sponsoring four projects:
1. the Psychic Sleuths Project, which examines the use of alleged psychics by law enforcement agencies;
2. the Anomaly Project, which deals with sightings of unidentified flying objects by scientists and engineers;
3. the Chinese Parapsychology Monitor, which promotes dialogue between U.S. parapsychologists and their colleagues in the People's Republic of China, and

4. the Soviet-U.S. Military Psi Research Monitor, which deals with the subject of this book.

The Center is interested in corresponding with individuals with information in any of these areas, and publishes a journal, the *Zetetic Scholar*. Subscriptions are $12.00 a year. The address is:

CSAR

P.O. Box 1052

Ann Arbor, Michigan 48103

PREFACE

WHEN I left private industry to join Jack Anderson's staff as an unpaid intern, it was not to write a book on parapsychology. My "beat" was the Department of State and the Middle East; occasionally I wrote about nuclear weapons or Pentagon cost overruns. I walked my beat on embassy row, collared military officers on subways, and subscribed to the professional military journals, which, like the subjects I covered, were not entertaining and don't sell much advertising.

Parapsychology, psychics, and the occult do sell advertising, but I never considered them "serious" topics, worthy of the sacrifices I had made to start a new career. I ignored rumors of a top secret "psychic task force" in a guarded Pentagon basement. When sources talked about the army's conceptual "First Earth Battalion" of psychic warrior monks, I changed the subject. Tanks, missiles, and budget overruns interested me. Psychics, warrior monks, and other fantasies did not.

In December 1980, my mind was changed. That month *Military Review,* the professional journal of the United States Army, featured an article entitled "The New Mental Battlefield: Beam Me Up Spock," by Lt. Col. John B. Alexander, complete with Kirlian photographs of the human "aura" on the cover. Alongside the usual articles like "The Deployment of the Pershing II to Europe—Some Implications" and "Preparing for War: Administrative Logistics Systems Program," Alexander's piece made some startling assertions:

- "There are weapons systems that operate on the power of the mind," he wrote, "and whose lethal capacity has already been demonstrated."
- "The ability to heal or cause disease can be transmitted over distance, thus inducing illness or death for no apparent cause. While this has been demonstrated on lower organisms, flies and frogs, the present capacity for human death is still debated."
- "The use of telepathic hypnosis also holds great [military] potential. This capability could allow agents to be deeply planted with no conscious knowledge of their programming."
- "Clearly, psychotronic weapons already exist; only their capabilities are in doubt."

I showed Alexander's article to Dale Van Atta, another Anderson associate who regularly covers the intelligence community. He too had heard rumors of the psychic task force. A trusted CIA source had recommended he read another article, this one by retired army Lt. Col. Thomas E. Bearden.

Bearden's article, "Soviet Psychotronic Weapons,"[1] made even Alexander sound like a Bible-thumping fundamentalist. Legionnaire's disease, he asserted, was induced by a Soviet "photonic barrier modulator," and another psychotronic weapon, the "hyperspace amplifier," sank the U.S. nuclear submarine *Thresher* in 1963 merely by concentrating psychic energies on its photograph.

I wasn't ready to submit such fantastic assertions to Jack Anderson on the basis of rumors and two articles in journals, but the more I looked, the more evidence I found that the United States and the Soviet Union took psychotronic weapons, weapons based on the psychic powers of the mind, seriously. The army does, indeed, have a conceptual First Earth Battalion of warrior monks, and its commander, Lt. Col. Jim Channon, encourages recruits to "join the army and learn ESP." The navy hires palm readers to track Soviet submarines. The National Security Agency has used psychics to break computer-generated codes. Both the Defense Intelligence Agency and the CIA have published reports warning that Soviet psychic breakthroughs might become "the atom bomb of espionage." Psychic researchers, I learned, included Nobel laureates and some of the most prestigious laboratories and universities in the world, including Stanford Research Institute and Princeton University.

When I finally brought a draft of my first psychic warfare column to Jack, his initial reaction was the same as mine—a flabbergasted look, and a plaintive, "Did you say 'warrior monks'?"

I had hoped that psychic warfare stories would not generate the unpleasant controversy that always surrounds my usual beat, the Middle East. Every article about that troubled area of the world brings in dozens of angry letters from one faction or another, all convinced that the report of certain "facts" can only result from sloppiness, bias, or worse. I was rudely awakened.

Letters poured in after the first Jack Anderson column on psychic warfare, and despite the column's references to "voodoo warfare" and "the juju team in the Pentagon's basement," only a few dozen objected to the reported $6 million budget for psychotronic weapons. An alarmed Baptist minister who wrote, "If the Soviets are doing it, so should we," spoke for the majority. Supporters of psychic research charged that either Mr. Anderson or myself was the unwitting victim of Soviet success in the field. We were, they said, acting under telepathic orders to discredit American research. *Fate* magazine suggested that our sources had "suspicious motives for wanting American psychotronic research stopped while the Soviets proceed with theirs."[2]

Critics of psychic research, while fewer in number, were no less vitriolic. *Discover* magazine proclaimed, "There has never been a shred of legitimate evidence for the existence of parapsychology," and urged, "millions for defense, but no cents for nonsense."[3] Magician and psychic-debunker James ("the Amazing") Randi declared that belief in the paranormal encourages fascism, and blamed psychic permissiveness for the mass suicide at Jim Jones's "People's Temple" in Guyana: "Such irrationalities lead to victims losing their sanity, their money, and sometimes their health and lives."[4]

Neither side lacks documentation for its claims, and the morass of conflicting allegations often makes it difficult, if not impossible, to determine the facts behind even the simplest report. Consider, for example, Lieutenant Colonel Alexander's article. He claims that microscopic examination of spoons and forks bent by Israeli psychic Uri Geller "has revealed a different form of fracturing than is experienced when metal items are ruptured by physical force," and refers to the eminent physicist John Taylor's book *Superminds*, published in 1975. Taylor himself cites electron microscope examinations by another physicist, Wilbur Franklin of Kent State University.

Long before Alexander's article, however, both Taylor and Franklin had recanted. Taylor's latest book, *Science and the Supernatural*, bitterly denounces all evidence of the paranormal as fakery, and shortly before his death in 1979, Franklin concluded that his microscopic studies were erroneous.

Franklin, I believe, died of natural causes, but in the rumor-ridden command centers of psychic warfare, there are those who would have us believe his death was:

1. suicide, in remorse for having lent aid and comfort to the purveyors of psychic snake oil, as has been claimed by skeptics, or
2. psychic attack by the Soviets, to prevent further U.S. advances in parapsychology, as has been claimed by psychic researchers, or
3. psychic attack by Americans, who are in reality under the control of a cabal of Tibetan Nazis headquartered in a Sufi monastery in Afghanistan. (This allegation didn't check out, although there really is a cabal of Argentinian Nazis at a Sufi monastery in Afghanistan.)

In the meantime, the torch of psychic metal-benders has been taken up by another eminent physicist, Dr. J. B. Hasted of the University of London. Hasted's tests have "reconfirmed" Franklin's initial findings.

It is difficult for a reporter to know who, what, when, where, or why to believe. Definitive documentation doesn't seem to exist. Within the government, and even within particular departments that have funded psychic research, dabbling in the occult generates witch-hunts. For example, some of the most interesting research has been funded by the navy. A former head of the Naval Electronics Systems Command in Washington, Dr. Joel S. Lawson, confessed that he has "thought ESP is the way to fight submarines" for twenty years, and was the government representative for two contracts with the Stanford Research Institute to test its feasibility. Today, Lawson isn't giving interviews, and the navy, according to official spokesmen, has not, does not, and will not test psychic submarine tracking.

Most people think of distant organizations like the navy as great monoliths, dominating Washington as mysteriously as Kafka's castle. In organizations closer to home, the local school board or the Tonawanda city government, people recognize the political complexities. There is always a tendency to ignore those complexities farther from home and to ascribe to organizations motivations that more properly belong only to a faction or even an individual within the organization. When the subject is parapsychology, that tendency can be fed by paranoid fears and grow to an obsession. I have letters from the alleged victims of CIA "psychic bullets" to prove it.

The situation is complicated further by the existence of numerous "special-interest groups" whose connections to the government are fuzzy at best. A number of the prominent psychic researchers, for example, belong to the U.S. Psychotronics Association, a private group interested in the development of psychic mechanisms like the "radionic shield," which supposedly protects the bearer from psychic attack. My first inclination would be to dismiss the bearers of radionic shields (which are energized when the user inserts a lock of his hair or a drop of blood) as nuts. In fact, however, a number of the association's members have documented contacts with the Pentagon, which even bought a radionic "multispectral image analyzer" in 1977 to track Soviet submarines. Several other members are respected scientists. Their claims, therefore, cannot be dismissed out of hand.

I have spent more than a year studying the conflicting reports, competing interest groups, and conjectures of psychic researchers. I cannot say with certainty that my conclusions really are the who, what, when, where, and how behind the rumors and allegations. I can promise that the facts in this book are the best I could produce and the most accurate record of these strange projects now available.

That difficulty—who, what, when, where, or why to believe—is one investigative reporters face more often than the average reader of a daily newspaper or viewer of the nightly news is likely to realize. The public is shielded from much of the controversy that surrounds the news. What you see and read usually reflects the conventional wisdom of the journalism community, which seldom resembles the consensus of experts (so seldom, in fact, that my first axiom of journalism is that anything factual is news to most people). There are exceptions to the conventional wisdom, of course, the true individualists such as Jack Anderson, but everyone sells advertising. Controversial views sell only when delivered in seriocomic wrappings, from pundits like William F. Buckley and William Safire, and do not have to be taken too seriously.

Reporters often hide behind something called "objectivity," for whose existence, in contrast to parapsychology, there really isn't a thread of legitimate evidence. No matter how dispassionately a story is covered, there is still subjectivity in the decision to place the story on page A1 or C30.

Investigative reporters exercise their subjectivity in deciding what to cover as well as how. No one reporter can devote equal

time and effort to natural gas prices, our dependence on foreign
oil, nuclear waste hazards, oil company profits, shoreline pollu-
tion, and the dozens of other issues that must be taken together
in an "objective" report on the energy crisis. I cover what interests
me, and my stories therefore reflect my preconceptions about
what is interesting.

The impossibility of truly objective reporting should not be
used as an excuse for wholesale abandonment of the facts, of
course. A reporter can record his version of reality. He can do so
better when both he and his readers are aware of the reporter's
preconceptions. These are mine:

I now accept the possibility of psychic phenomena, although
I find the research now available far from convincing. If psychic
phenomena do exist, they will revolutionize science, and I therefore support modest government funding of such research.

I have tried to avoid judging specific programs on the merit of
the science involved. I am not competent to judge science. Some
research programs have clearly been fraudulent, but I have judged
them so only when there was clear evidence of fraud outside of
the apparent unlikelihood of a particular theory.

I have also tried to avoid falling into conspiracy theories. My
experience as an investigative reporter has taught me that there
are many people who conspire, but few conspiracies.

I have tried to let the evidence, and the researchers who were
willing to talk on the record, speak for themselves. Sometimes
that evidence is difficult to judge. Just how difficult the evidence
of one's senses can be I learned while writing this book.

Because my own conclusions are fallible, I have given some of
the main characters in my story the opportunity to review the
manuscript and suggest revisions. In almost every case, I accepted
those revisions.

So many people have aided me in the writing of this book that
it is impossible to acknowledge them all here. First among them,

of course, is Jack Anderson, as well as Joe Spear, Jack's column editor, and Dale Van Atta, the associate who taught me most of what I know about investigative reporting. I should also like to thank here Marcello Truzzi, Dr. Stanley R. Dean, *Apollo 14* astronaut Edgar D. Mitchell, James ("the Amazing") Randi, Randy Fitzgerald, John Wilhelm, Alan Gevins, Jack Sarfatti, Anita and Filipo Tellez (owners of Anita's, the best Mexican restaurant in the Washington, D.C. area), Edward Panek, and, for wielding "the whip," Sue Merrow.

NOTES

1. *Specula,* March–June 1978.
2. *Fate,* July 1981, p. 92.
3. "Skeptical Eye," *Discover,* March 1981.
4. *Flim-Flam,* p. 256.

INTRODUCTION BY JACK ANDERSON

As a confessed muckraker, I hold no security clearance. Most government officials, if possible, avoid me. The mere mention of my name has caused them to shut their doors and lock their files. Yet I am privy to some of the most sensitive information in their vaults. I have regular access to documents so secret that the classification stamps themselves are classified.

Early in 1981, my associate Ron McRae and I revealed a Pentagon secret that raised eyebrows from coast to coast. To the skeptics who wrote in, no, we don't take hallucinogens. The Pentagon and the Kremlin are, indeed, dabbling in the black arts.

They are seriously trying to develop weapons based on extrasensory perception. If the research is successful, the next war could presumably be won by weapons like the "hyperspatial nuclear howitzer," which can supposedly transmit a nuclear explosion from the Nevada desert to the gates of the Kremlin with the speed of thought, or the "photonic barrier modulator," which, like a voodoo doll, can induce death or illness telepathically from thousands of miles away.

By Pentagon standards, not much money has been invested in psychic warfare, but the commanders of the top secret psychic task force who oversee the research think we should be spending a lot more.

Congressman Charlie Rose (D–N.C.), a respected six-term congressman and member of the House Select Committee on Intelligence, worries that Soviet research, which the intelligence community estimates at $30 million a year, might open a "psychic arms gap."

"They could make every other weapon obsolete," Rose asserts.

The congressman is quite correct: The Buck Rogers weapons will certainly make plain old nuclear weapons obsolete—if they should ever work. One such weapon is an antimissile system that would throw a time warp over the North Pole. Incoming Soviet missiles would fly into the warp and explode harmlessly in the past; if the time warp mechanism was tuned to a really high frequency, it might kill a few dinosaurs.

It would be a mistake, however, to relegate all these projects to the comic books. Adm. William Leahy made that mistake during World War II, declaring, "The A-bomb is the biggest fool thing we have ever done. . . . The bomb will never go off, and I speak as an expert on explosives."

I cannot speak as an expert on explosives, quantum mechanics, cybernetics, or any of the other technologies critical to the investigation of parapsychology. Some of these investigations have the potential for important scientific advances.

I can speak as an expert on reporting what goes on inside the Pentagon, however. No reporter wishes to interfere with legitimate military research. Alongside comic-book projects like the antimissile time warp over the North Pole, there are laboratories on the threshold of discovering the secrets of the human mind. Like the discovery of atomic fission almost half a century ago, these discoveries have the potential to benefit mankind—or to destroy it.

Then why tell the secrets? Admittedly, newsmen are not security experts, and the publication of military secrets is always a thorny question. What qualifies a reporter to judge whether military research is a waste of money or a scientific breakthrough? Certainly I am not competent to outguess the Joint Chiefs. I do not claim to know infallibly whether a military venture is bound to end in catastrophe. I cannot say, on my own authority, that psychics can't plot the movements of Soviet missile submarines off the coast of California as well as sonar-equipped ships and aircraft. Nor can I assert, as a scientist, that attempts to destroy Soviet satellites by telepathy are a waste of money. But I am in close touch with military experts and scientists whom the Joint Chiefs themselves consult. With their help, I can often give the people an alternative to the official version of things, a rival account of reality, a measure by which to judge the efficacy of rulers and whether the truth is in them. At the risk of appearing immodest, I think my record proves the need for that alternative.

Information is power, and the political and military leaders in Washington would like to keep it in their own hands. One of the irreversible currents I have noted in thirty-four years of reporting is the hankering of our leaders to transform themselves from servants into sovereigns. Any information, from the planned budget for energy conservation to intelligence reports on Soviet psychic breakthroughs, can serve to make some bureaucrat feel a little more powerful than those who aren't "cleared" for the secret.

The Pentagon has been as uncooperative as usual since we uncovered the psychic task force. The navy at first denied it had employed psychics to track Soviet submarines, and then refused to comment when one of the sub-chasing swamis appeared on a New York television show. The head of the psychic task force, Army Assistant Chief of Staff for Intelligence Major General Thompson, first promised and then canceled an interview, and finally claimed through a spokesman that he had nothing to do with voodoo warfare. Cooperative officials were ordered to keep quiet.

The budget for psychic research, I have said, is small by Pentagon standards, but the revelations of my columns and this book raise larger issues. If psychic research is successful, and the laws of physics as we now understand them overturned, who will control this new knowledge? Will the uses of psychic discoveries be publicly debated or decided in the secrecy of the intelligence agencies? Have Soviet psychics penetrated the security of the

United States, and have we entered an era, when, in the words of Congressman Rose, "there are no secrets"? What if the "photonic barrier modulator" and the "hyperspatial nuclear howitzer" are as loony as they sound? What do these projects say about the officials who supervise these projects, men near the pinnacle of the national security establishment? These issues can only be resolved when reporters have the will and the means to tear down the curtains of official secrecy.

But the way an investigative reporter is compelled to answer these questions, of course, has always been an imperfect system of news gathering. Investigative reporters must work harder, dig deeper, and verify the facts more carefully than reporters who follow the official line. Sometimes the sources do not have all the details. Sometimes the jigsaw pieces of information do not form a complete picture and the missing pieces are buried too deeply. Investigative reporters must work without the power of subpoena. They lack the money and manpower that the government can muster to counter their efforts. Nevertheless, with hard work and a little luck, they can succeed.

Ron McRae knows investigative journalism from inside and out. For several years, he was one of those "unauthorized sources" within the government I have always depended on. In 1979, he came in from the cold and joined my staff as an intern. Since then, he has become one of the best investigators in the business.

MIND WARS

1 · MADAME ZODIAC

THE sign on the modest storefront reads, MADAME ZODIAC, PSYCHIC. PALMS READ, HOROSCOPES INTERPRETED. Madame Zodiac's Washington, D.C., parlor opens at eleven, and many of her regular customers have their readings during the lunch break. The usual charge is ten dollars.

For eleven months during 1979 and 1980, Madame's parlor opened early every third Tuesday for a special customer. A little after nine, a navy commander, discreetly dressed in a civilian suit and carrying a government briefcase handcuffed to his wrist, was ushered into the private parlor. Madame made tea while the commander, pushing aside her crystal ball and tarot cards, spread photographs and charts on the table.

The commander fumbled for a cigarette. He was down to half a pack a day that June, but hadn't been able to quit. "You'll quit by the end of the year," Madame predicted.

That prediction proved accurate, and the commander is now running six miles a day and hopes to compete in the next Marine Corps marathon. But he didn't give Madame Zodiac an envelope stuffed with four hundred dollars cash every month to help himself break the nicotine habit. The visits to Madame Zodiac were official. The money came from the Office of Naval Intelligence, and the photographs and charts on the table were of Soviet submarines and their estimated tracks off the eastern coast of the United States. Madame Zodiac's mission: use her psychic powers to do what the navy's ships and aircraft sometimes could not do —track the Soviet missile subs and predict their maneuvers.

Madame Zodiac is a pseudonym, since her contract with the

navy included a secrecy agreement. The navy has employed at least thirty-four psychics to track Soviet ships and submarines. One who agreed to have her name published is Shawn Robbins (a professional psychic rated as one of the nation's "top ten" by the *National Enquirer*, in which Robbins predicted that "after learning that the Soviet Union plans to use psychic weapons against the United States, the government will dump millions of dollars into crash psychic research.")[1] She also predicted that "a poltergeist, a mischievous ghost, will startle the White House by shattering ornaments and making loud noises."

In 1973, Robbins was one of the experimental subjects for a psychic research program at the prestigious Maimonides Medical Center in New York. In a typical experiment, subjects viewed "emotionally arousing" or erotic films while others attempted to learn the contents of the film telepathically. As they slept after the films, the electrical activity of the subjects' brains were monitored to detect the periods of rapid eye movement (called REM sleep) associated with dreaming. The sleepers were awakened and asked to describe their dreams, and the responses of those who had actually seen the films and those who had received telepathic communications were compared. Robbins's dreams correlated with the contents of the films as well as those who had actually seen them, indicating, according to the research team, extraordinary psychic abilities.

Shortly after testing at the hospital ended, Robbins was contacted by a man she had known previously as an officer of the private foundation that funded the study. He identified himself as a commander from the Office of Naval Intelligence. The navy was interested in testing Robbins's psychic abilities against Soviet naval targets. Robbins agreed and, like Madame Zodiac, was given charts and photographs of Soviet ships and asked to locate them and predict their movements.

"He said I did well," Robbins claims, "and he wanted to do more tests." Robbins declined because of a previous commitment to go treasure hunting in Greece.

Seven years later, the same navy commander asked Robbins to participate in the Madame Zodiac Project, and tested her again. Although Robbins scored well, reductions in the Reagan budget cut her out of the program.

Eight years after the Maimonides experiments ended, researcher Stanley Krippner learned that the "private" foundation funding his work had acted as a front for the CIA.

Madame Zodiac is what the Pentagon might call a "medium technological risk" project: not exactly conservative, but not as farfetched as some others.

The navy began serious parapsychology research in World War II. Many of the projects involved "an-psi," or the alleged psychic powers of animals, and were pragmatically directed to the problems of the day. One small project attempted to train or psychically direct sea gulls to defecate on the periscopes of German submarines. A more ambitious study, headed by Dr. J. Gaither Pratt of Duke University, hoped to discover a psychic navigation mechanism in homing pigeons that would enable submarines to navigate without surfacing or bombers to locate German targets at night, when they were less vulnerable to German fighters. The navy continued to fund psychic research at Duke through the sixties.

An-psi still interests government scientists. The U.S. Geological Survey pays volunteers in California to watch animals for early warning signs of earthquakes. Project scientists theorize that rocks under pressure emit positive ions a few days before an earthquake. Positive ions drive both humans and animals wild—the crime rate in California jumps whenever the ion-laden Santa Ana winds blow, but the scientists hope the animals will prove even more reliable than monitoring machines. China, the only nation with any claim to success in predicting earthquakes, has monitored animals for years, and credits the program with saving one hundred thousand lives.

By far the weirdest project funded by any government agency

is the "multispectral image analyzer station" the navy bought from Virginia Beach chiropractor and psychic Charles Whitehouse in 1977. Whitehouse is a board member of the U.S. Psychotronics Association, Inc. (USPA), an organization producing equipment that supposedly amplifies psychic energies by use of electronic devices. Whitehouse assured the head of photographic research and development for the navy, Capt. Robert Skillen (now retired), that they could locate a Soviet submarine simply by inserting a photograph of it into the machine.

"It is possible to detect a submarine this way," Skillen asserts. Whitehouse trained several persons from Skillen's department and the CIA to operate the machine, and the navy shelled out $5,111 for the little black box. "The work that Whitehouse did was creditable," says Skillen. "He did move into the area [where the submarine was]. And we did come back and buy this little gee-whiz machine. And he did train several of my people—people who have been previously involved with the CIA."

Whitehouse still proudly displays the check stub and receipt for "one multispectral image analyzer station." Whitehouse also used the machine to treat cancer patients at his chiropractic clinic, correcting "holes" and "imbalances" in the patients' auras (an invisible psychic halo) by shining various combinations of colored lights on their body. Any malady can be cured by the proper combination of lights, Whitehouse claims, and the analyzer's technical manual even lists the cure for "bombs (A and hydrogen)." The machine won't work unless operated from a pedestal at least three feet off the ground "to avoid the polarizing influence of cosmic rays."

Civil defense and the air force showed no interest in a machine that could cure the A-bomb, but the Virginia board of medical ethics did. Board investigators accused the doctor of defrauding patients. Whitehouse immigrated to Thailand, where, he hopes, "life will be more leisurely," and avoided prosecution.

Purchases like the multispectral image analyzer cast a shadow over all psychic research, of course, but antisubmarine warfare is exactly the sort of problem that has proved intractable for conventional technology and where, therefore, unconventional approaches stand to gain the most. Not all the new approaches to antisubmarine warfare are psychic; the navy is testing blimps too, and some engineers think the blimp's low speed, noise, and long endurance make it ideal for dipping sonar and listening patiently for submarines. Blimps appall the carrier admirals, but they're cheap, so some research survives the opposition.

Antisubmarine ESP has its fervent advocates too. The former head of the Naval Electronic Systems Command in Washington, D.C., Dr. Joel S. Lawson, Jr., confesses that he has thought "ESP is the way to fight submarines for twenty years." Psychics cost even less than blimps and seem likely to endure their critics too.

The primary effect of the opposition to ongoing psychic programs in the Pentagon has been to change the names to protect those guilty of such research. A $100,000 1978 CIA study on Soviet ESP never mentions the word *psychic* and uses the pseudo-technical circumlocution, "novel biological information transfer systems," to avoid mentioning ESP. The navy public affairs branch flatly denies it does or ever has "used psychics to track submarines" and passed off even the most technically low risk of the psychic antisubmarine projects, an $87,000 contract between the Naval Electronic Systems Command and the prestigious Stanford Research Institute begun in 1976 and completed in 1978, as "an investigation of the ability of certain individuals to perceive remote faint electromagnetic stimuli at a noncognitive level of awareness." In plain English, "certain individuals" may perceive "remote faint electromagnetic stimuli," that is, a flashing light in another room (in the experiment) or the engines of a submerged submarine, at a "noncognitive level of awareness," that is, psychically, without thinking about it. The lengthy project report never mentions the word *psychic*, although the researchers, Harold Puthoff and Russell Targ, are perhaps the world's best-known physicists in the field of psychic research, and the *certain individuals*, professional psychics.

Are they serious? Can the Pentagon really believe that palm readers can track submarines or that psychic agents can hypnotize American generals? Individuals disagree. According to Lieutenant Colonel Alexander, some people will consider the information in his *Military Review* article on the psychic battlefield ridiculous, "since it does not conform to their view of reality, but some people still believe the world is flat." Others view sub-tracking swamis as a conservative approach, compared to antimissile time warps that will send Soviet missiles hurtling into the dinosaur era.

There are individuals in top defense posts who take psychic warfare very seriously indeed. Dr. Lawson, for one, continues to address the need for psychic research despite quiet and, until now, unofficial reprimands. So far the advocates have not convinced the Pentagon to devote large amounts of money to psychic research.

Psychic research may get $6 million annually, probably somewhat less. Reliable figures are unavailable, in part because much of the research is hidden in the secret intelligence budget, and in part because even unclassified programs are disguised by titles such as "Novel Biological Information Transfer." The budget for psychic research, however, might underrepresent its importance. Psychic research more resembles research on laser "death ray" weapons, which some claim will orbit the earth and zap intercontinental missiles before they reenter the atmosphere. The budget for laser weapons in 1982 was slightly under $50 million, pocket change at the Pentagon, where a single modern airplane can cost $250 million, a single ship $1.5 billion, and a major weapons program such as the MX missile, $66 billion plus.

Obviously a technological breakthrough in either laser weapons or psychic warfare could swing the balance of the cold war. Although he would probably resent the comparison, the former director of Air Force Intelligence, Gen. George Keegan, like the advocates of psychic warfare, insists the Soviets far outstrip the United States in his chosen field, laser weapons. Most engineers disagree. As is the case with psychic weapons, the technological

barriers to laser weapons are greater than nonspecialists are inclined to believe after watching "Star Trek" reruns.

So far, there is no technological breakthrough in either field.
Laser researchers at least know what to look for. Pointing a pencil-
thin laser beam at a supersonic missile across thousands of miles
of space may be a nearly impossible engineering problem, but the
physics that underlie the problem can be found in a high school
text. Psychic researchers don't have a text and can't even prove
to everyone's satisfaction that psychic phenomena exist.

Critics have attacked projects that attempt to apply parapsychology to practical problems, such as tracking submarines, on the
grounds that you cannot build up applications of a science until
that science and its theoretical foundations have been established.
You cannot apply parapsychology unless psychic powers exist, and
applied pseudoscience is worse than plain pseudoscience because
it sells snake oil remedies. Yet the claims of psychic advocates, at
least on the surface, are impressive. What if Madame Zodiac
really does find Soviet submarines?

Sociologist Marcello Truzzi suggests a distinction between "experimental parapsychology" and "clinical parapsychology" similar
to the distinction between experimental and clinical psychology.
The criteria for evaluating clinical efforts is far broader than the
purely scientific criteria found in experimental methods. Good
clinical methods are methods that work. Whether the theory is
correct or not does not matter; what matters is whether the
patient improves or the submarine is found.

"The existence of psychic powers might have extremely important military-political consequences should the enemy be able to
use it to break through national security defenses," warns Truzzi.
Even if the chances are small that such powers really exist, "It is
simply too important to neglect."[2]

Many self-proclaimed psychics' claims for effectiveness prove
to be invalid. The secrecy of intelligence research as well as official
reluctance to admit to dabbling in the black arts make it particularly difficult to validate the claims for Madame Zodiac and the

other military projects that have been revealed. There are public
records available, however, that can cast some light on these
claims: the records of public police departments.

Truzzi heads a research team doing the most comprehensive
survey ever of the employment of psychics in criminal investigations. "We're only in the first phase of a several-phase project,"
he says, "but we're already finding that psychics have been used
more than anyone realized."

The use of psychics by police departments in criminal investigations closely parallels hoped-for military applications. Police
search for missing persons and evidence, and intelligence agencies
for hidden agents and bases. Both the CIA and the Los Angeles
police would like to read the minds of informers and suspects. If
the police find psychics useful, so, probably, will the Pentagon,
whether or not anyone understands the theory behind the effect.

The police chief of Bridgewater Township, New Jersey, knew
what he thought of psychics. "Quite frankly," says Chief Dix
Fetzer, "I thought they were bunk." But Fetzer was a desperate
man. His investigation of the most brutal murder in Bridgewater's
history was at a dead end, and Peter Hurkos, the Dutch "Radar
Brain Man," legendary for his psychic aid to the anti-Nazi underground during World War II, had offered to help.

Today, Fetzer thinks differently. "Hurkos," he says, "furnished
us with a preponderance of leads that were not obtainable with
conventional investigative techniques." The gun, used in the
crime Hurkos had predicted, would be found hidden in the wall
at the murder site. The police tore apart the wall without finding
the weapon, but a year later it was found hidden in the wall of
another building. Hurkos did even better, according to Chief
Fetzer: "Using his unbelievable powers, Hurkos provided us with
the identity of the perpetrator, by first and last name." Two years
later, an accomplice confessed, and the suspect named by Hurkos
was brought to trial.

"I would recommend Hurkos without qualification," Chief Fetzer asserts.

Despite this ringing endorsement, Elliot Ness is still in and Madame Zodiac still out of most squad rooms. Police officials tend to view psychic sleuths with something less than enthusiasm, and even in Bridgewater, only Chief Fetzer would comment on the record. The Atlanta task force investigating the murder of black children considered the thirteen hundred letters it got from would-be psychic detectives an annoyance. But desperate men will try anything once, and even Atlanta eventually consulted psychic Dorothy Allison. Allison later claimed her psychic impressions were valid, but police officials in Atlanta characterized her clues as "vague" and "unhelpful." Other police departments have been favorably impressed by Allison, however.

Psychics are not yet commonly used in investigations, but they are winning converts at federal, state, and local law enforcement agencies. The Department of Justice of the state of California has even issued standard operating procedures for "the use of psychics in investigations."

"It does appear that psychics have provided valuable assistance to law enforcement," according to the California procedures. "A talented psychic can assist [investigators] by helping to:

· locate the geographic area of a missing person,
· narrow the number of leads to be concentrated on,
· highlight information that has been overlooked, or
· provide information previously unknown to the investigator."

The California procedures warn that "even talented psychics cannot be accurate 100 percent of the time." Psychics do not replace sound police work, but they do "function as an investigative tool."

Other studies support that conclusion. An article entitled

"Managing the Psychic in Criminal Investigations" in *Police Chief* magazine, the official publication of the International Association of Chiefs of Police, said "individuals with bona fide psychic ability offer a unique and potentially valuable investigative skill."[3] In 1982, Stanford Research Institute published the first scientific and very favorable study of psychic detectives. Another favorable study by two experienced criminologists, Whitney S. Hubbard and Raymond W. Worring, is *Psychic Criminology: An Operations Manual for Using Psychics in Criminal Investigations.*

Although many police officials are reluctant to discuss psychic sleuths, psychics are not only consulted by but are even staff members of some departments. In San Jose, California, Clarissa Bernhardt, a psychic known as "the Earthquake Lady" for her predictions of tremors, is an officer of the San Jose Search and Rescue Team. "I don't know how she does it," says Director George Andrews, "but we're very happy to have her. Her psychic powers have solved at least two cases for us." She may have solved a third case too, but the Federal Aviation Administration refused to send scuba divers to search for a missing plane Bernhardt felt had crashed into a lake, with nothing more than the psychic's word to go on. The aircraft was never found.

By official invitation, Bernhardt has taught search and rescue teams all over California how to use "the hunch factor" to locate missing persons. "I am interested in bringing more respect to the field of parapsychology," she says. "People often prefer to look the other way."

The psychic investigators themselves have organized. Astronaut Edgar Mitchell formed a "psychic posse" in an attempt to find heiress Patricia Hearst after her kidnapping by the Symbionese Liberation Army. In Saint Louis, police asked the United States Psi Squad (a wholly private organization, with no connection to the federal government; *psi* is short for "psychic") to help last year in the case of a father of seven who disappeared during a chess tournament. Police found only the man's truck and glasses.

The Psi Squad met at the home of its leader, Beverly Jaegers, a suburban housewife and mother of six. The squad includes a lawyer, policemen, a retired real estate salesman, and several pilots, twenty members in all. Pilots are the best male psychics, says Jaegers, because "no matter how much instrumentation they have, they always fly by the seat of their pants." Most psychic detectives are women.

With two Saint Louis detectives taping the session, the squad members reported their impressions from a picture of the missing man: a missing right hubcap, one headlight out, a desolate salvage yard, a dead phone in a nearby booth, a large belt buckle. The police confirmed these details. The truck was missing a right hubcap and headlight, the man wore a large belt buckle, and there was a salvage yard and phone booth near where the truck was found. One detective tore a photograph of the man and his wife in half and placed it face down in Beverly Jaegers' hand. The half with the man's image felt cold.

The United States Psi Squad did not pinpoint the location of the body, and the man is still listed officially as missing. Police in Saint Louis credit them with providing crucial leads in other cases, however.

Another group is the Society for Psychic Investigation, Inc., which, according to its literature, offers services to "law enforcement organizations throughout the United States and Canada." Periodic society bulletins supply members with photographs, facts, and a case questionnaire. Responses are tabulated by a computer, which also reports back to psychics on how well they answered.

Neither group accepts payment for its services, other than expenses. The California procedures warn against psychics who are "more interested in notoriety or money than in solving the case. Many psychics who are primarily interested in using their ability to help others wish to remain anonymous."

Some of the private psychic organizations are more concerned with military than police applications of parapsychology. The

Messiah Survival Center, headquartered in Philadelphia, has organized a nationwide network of telepaths to replace conventional long-distance communication systems, which would presumably be destroyed by a nuclear war. Psychic backup for
communications has been officially investigated by both the Soviet and U.S. governments. According to the Defense Intelligence Agency, "There are reports that the Soviets are training
their cosmonauts in telepathy to back up their electronic equipment while in outer space. One of these backup schemes is known
to involve coded telepathic messages," to prevent interception by
American intelligence. During the *Apollo 14* moon flight, astronaut Edgar Mitchell tried without success to send messages to a
telepathic receiver in Dallas. Despite Mitchell's failure, in 1976
NASA bought an "ESP teaching machine" from University of
California at Davis parapsychologist Charles Tart, a well known
researcher in altered states of consciousness. The device was
tested at NASA's Jet Propulsion Lab and later at Stanford Research Institute under a navy contract, with inconclusive results.

Courts, of course, do not accept the testimony of psychics, so
police must still prove their cases with standard investigative
procedures. Many policemen remain skeptical.

Two studies conducted by the Behavioral Sciences Section of
the Los Angeles Police Department failed to replicate the positive
results obtained by psychic sleuths in other studies. In one test,
psychics were asked to identify twenty-one key aspects of a case,
such as the victim's name or age, from a personal sample such as
a lock of hair or key chain. No psychic named more than six
factors correctly, and the typical score was two or three.

Like military research, police interest in the psychic ranges
from the mundane to the bizarre. For example, hypnosis is widely
used to enhance witnesses' recall and is so commonly accepted
that few would characterize it as a "psychic" phenomenon. In
fact, however, scientists aren't sure what hypnosis is; most of the
early scientific studies were carried out by parapsychology investigators and spiritualists who believed entranced persons have

heightened psychic powers. The tinge of spiritualism remains, and conventional psychologists often still feel uncomfortable with the concept of hypnosis and prefer to ignore it. Police are enthusiastic, perhaps dangerously so, according to recent research by University of Pennsylvania psychiatrist Martin T. Orne. Hypnotized persons, says Dr. Orne, tend to have diminished critical judgment and are highly responsive to even unconscious suggestions furnished by the hypnotist.

"If the hypnotist has beliefs about what the witness or victim might have seen or about who the guilty person might be, it is all too easy for these beliefs to be transferred into the memories of responsive hypnotic subjects," Orne says. Likewise, the subject's own beliefs about the crime may be converted into "pseudomemories," which the witness will believe and swear to be true. Courts allow police to interrogate witnesses under hypnosis, but are beginning to put restrictions on the practice.

The Soviets are even more inclined to accept hypnosis, according to the Defense Intelligence Agency. "In the Soviet Union, hypnotism is a common tool like X rays, used in medicine, physiology, and psychology," as well as police investigations: "Hypnotizing someone telepathically probably comes over as a more eerie, mystifying, even diabolical act in the United States than it does in the Soviet Union."

On the other end of the spectrum, and by all odds the most bizarre research ever undertaken by both the military and police agencies, is the "Backster effect"—plants reading human minds. Cleve Backster was a polygraph operator who claimed to have discovered that a plant attached to a lie detector will "faint" if someone thinks about plucking a leaf, and vegetables' growth will languish if they take a dislike to the gardener. Many amateur horticulturists have long suspected things like this, but Backster actually attempted to prove it by "interrogating," with the cooperation of the New York City Police Department, a plant that had been present at a murder. The police were persuaded to parade twenty suspects past the plant, but the leafy witness was unable to finger a suspect. Later the Backster effect was investigated by the CIA and the navy—you can see the devastating effect this would have: Smuggle a psychic philodendron into the Kremlin's council chambers, and their darkest secrets would be ours.

Truzzi compares the more conventional uses of psychics to police employment of psychiatrists. "Both are used to draw profiles of potential suspects," he says, and "to some degree, both are flying by the seat of their pants."

But don't expect psychics to witness confessions or testify alongside psychiatric witnesses anytime soon. Psychics have undoubtably aided police with "unbelievable powers" or lucky guesses or maybe just common sense. But even in Bridgewater Township, where Peter Hurkos named the suspect brought to trial "by first and last name," their contribution is controversial. The suspect Hurkos named and Chief Fetzer charged was acquitted. Chief Fetzer blamed a "liberal judge"; the defense called the evidence circumstantial and inconclusive. Hurkos's legendary psychic adventures with the World War II Dutch underground turned out to be just that—legend.

Whether or not one believes Hurkos, it is a fact that police all over the country are consulting psychics in life-and-death situations. Tomorrow, someone might live or die because Clarissa Bernhardt guesses to send the San Jose Search and Rescue Team north instead of east, and that possibility gives psychic sleuths an importance that transcends the few thousand dollars an individual police department might spend to support them. To be fair to the practitioners of "clinical parapsychology," there is a lot of guesswork to searches and no good reason to reject one guess in favor of another.

Some police departments publicize psychics despite their skepticism about their effectiveness. Truzzi's survey has discovered instances in which the well-publicized arrival of a psychic sleuth panicked the perpetrators, and in some cases even caused a suspect who believed in their powers to confess.

The Pentagon has likewise sought to capitalize on the superstitious beliefs of the enemy. During the Communist-inspired Huk rebellion in the Philippines in the early fifties, a team of CIA operatives circulated a rumor that a dread *asuange,* a vampire, roamed the Communist region. To lend the rumor credibility, the agents ambushed a rebel patrol, snatched the last man, severed his jugular with two vampirelike punctures, and hung him upside down until his blood drained out. The insurgents found the body lying on a trail, and since these Communists were as superstitious as most Filipinos, hundreds fled. More recently, the CIA considered using special fireworks to convince Cubans that the heavens had opened and the messiah was on his way to oust the atheistic Communists.

But does interest in the paranormal go beyond a desire to capitalize on superstition? Is the Pentagon as serious about psychics as the San Jose Search and Rescue Team or the Department of Justice of the state of California? Not if we accept official protestations that Madame Zodiac, the multispectral image analyzer, and the detection of faint electromagnetic stimuli "at a noncognitive level of awareness" at the prestigious Stanford Research Institute laboratories can all be lumped together as anomalies that fell through the cracks in the administrative review process.

There are excellent reasons to believe that the advocates of psychic warfare have more influence in the Pentagon than has been admitted, however, besides the thirty-year record of psychic research in the CIA, the army, navy, air force, and Marine Corps, NASA, the Defense Intelligence Agency, the National Institute of Health, and, in fact, just about every conceivable government agency. More convincing still, the Pentagon itself has consulted psychics in the same sort of life-and-death situations faced by search and rescue teams.

During the Vietnam War, the Marine Corps deployed a platoon of dowsers with the I Corps near Hue, one of the most dangerous combat zones of the war. The platoon was trained to locate hidden tunnels and weapons caches with Y-shaped wire dowsing rods at the Marine Corps Training and Development Command at Quantico, near Washington, D.C. After five months, the platoon was withdrawn, not, according to a letter from the commander of the Training and Development Command, because they had been unsuccessful in the combat tests, but because the successful use of dowsing appeared to require "special skills that cannot be taught to the average marine."

Another operational test of parapsychology was more recent and had more in common with police employment of psychics, although dowsers have been used by police to search for evidence such as a murder weapon discarded at a dump. The Defense Department used psychics in an attempt to find General Dozier, kidnapped by the Italian Red Brigades in January 1982.[4] On five occasions, the American embassy in Rome relayed psychic tips from the Pentagon to Italy's elite antiterrorist police. One medium visualized a quiet farmhouse near Verona with a river running nearby and even described the room in which she believed Dozier was held. Italian police raided at gunpoint a number of houses that fitted the psychic's description and in one surprised a prominent Italian businessman who had hoped to spend a quiet weekend with a lady friend. Other raids prompted by psychic leads were similarly unsuccessful.

Dozier was eventually rescued, apparently hours before his scheduled execution, thanks to a massive investigation and the arrest of hundreds of suspected Red Brigades sympathizers. The key leads came from drug pushers who traded immunity from prosecution for information about customers of the Red Brigades. In these circumstances, it is remarkable that the Pentagon thought enough of psychics to divert the very limited resources of the Italian antiterrorist squad to check psychic leads.

Although Pentagon spokesmen resolutely refuse to confirm or deny the existence of specific psychic warfare projects, advocates feel freer to talk since the Reagan administration.

According to Barbara Honegger, who came into the White House with former chief presidential domestic adviser Martin Anderson, and worked three years in the Office of Policy Development, the Reagan administration is aware of the latest achievements in parapsychology "at the highest levels of the Office of Science and Technology Policy, the Office of Policy Development, and the National Security Council."

Honegger, who has published her own parapsychology research in several journals, claims that parapsychology played a major role in one of the administration's most controversial defense decisions—abandoning the Carter administration's "shell-game" deployment for the MX missile. Carter proposed shifting each MX missile among as many as twenty individual concrete shelters. Soviet planners, Carter hoped, could never know which shelter to target, and the MX missile could therefore survive any Soviet first strike.

According to Honegger, "Prominent U.S. psi researchers have been funded by the government to conduct studies whose results have clear applicability to the enhanced predictability of mobile MX missile locations." In other words, U.S. studies show Soviet psychics could beat the shell game and pinpoint the missiles. Honegger even claims Soviet psychics might pinpoint the missiles before they are moved: "If the United States installs the shell-game version of the [MX] system, a potential aggressor need only utilize a precognitive strategy that can more accurately determine the future location of the missiles, at a specified time in the future corresponding to the amount of time it takes for a missile to leave its launch pad and arrive at a destination in the United States."

Congressman Charlie Rose, a ranking member of the House Special Committee on Intelligence, echoes Honegger's concern. Rose suggested the Soviets might use dowsing rods deployed in satellites—SADDOR, for "satellite deployed dowsing rod"—to pinpoint the missiles.

A January 1982 article in *Signal,* the journal of the Armed

Forces Communications and Electronics Association, also noted
the strategic potential of parapsychology. According to Roger A.
Beaumont, a military historian at Texas A&M University, "Interest in the military potential of ESP has grown in recent years."

Beaumont admits the interest may be a ruse. "Nations involved
in disarmament talks may interject 'jokers' or 'riders' into otherwise serious and rational proposals to make sure that their opponents will not accept them. Those thus maneuvered into the role
of rejectors may then seem in the eyes of the technically unaware
public to be the foes of peace. A corollary to this is the strategy
of shadow programs to draw an adversary's attention—and resources—into a dead end, the essence of Soviet efforts in the field
of disinformation."

We know that at least some of the research, however, both in
the Soviet Union and the United States, is legitimate, not disinformation. Certainly, the Pentagon would not have endangered
General Dozier with phony psychic leads merely to confuse the
Soviets. And Pentagon psychic sleuths are searching even today
for another group the Pentagon would dearly like to see returned
alive—the MIAs (missing in action) from the Vietnam War.

Navy Capt. Joseph L. Dick leads the Defense Intelligence
Agency team responsible for gathering the slender evidence that
a few of the MIAs might be alive. Psychics, he says, have been
given bits of aircraft or articles of clothing, anything that might
establish a telepathic link with the MIAs.

"Some of their leads have checked out," according to Captain
Dick. "They've been able to visualize aircraft crashes, and we've
found the wreckage where they indicated." None of the evidence
is conclusive, although several of the psychics have claimed telepathic contact with MIAs imprisoned in Cambodian jungle
camps.

Captain Dick also feels the meditation and relaxation techniques used by psychics may produce better, more alert soldiers.
"There is a lot of official interest in these relaxation techniques,"
according to Dick, "at the highest levels."

Should the Pentagon wish to expand its stable of psychic sleuths, it will find psychics easier to recruit than soldiers. In February 1981, the American embassy in Rome was besieged by hundreds of callers volunteering to track Soviet submarines. Flabbergasted embassy officials found that an English scandal sheet had picked up the recently published story of Madame Zodiac and added some flourishes of its own. The Pentagon, claimed the paper, was "consulting top British psychics and spiritualists . . . apparently to urge them to use their powers against the Kremlin."[5]

NOTES

1. *National Enquirer,* January 3, 1982.
2. *Zetetic Scholar,* Spring 1982.
3. *Police Chief,* May 1979.
4. First reported by Pierre Salinger on ABC "World News To-night."
5. *London Sun,* March 12, 1982.

2 · THE NEED TO
BELIEVE

"I should rather believe the gentlemen lied," President Thomas Jefferson reportedly said, "than believe that stones fell from the sky." Thus ended the first government investigation of unidentified flying objects more than 160 years before the air force closed the books on Project Blue Book.

The gentlemen returned to Harvard. The meteorites Jefferson sent them to investigate stayed buried on a Vermont farm. The question of how the government, the public, and other scientists should react to evidence that challenges the conventional wisdom remains. Scientists and presidents, it seems, are no less troubled than investigative reporters or the police when confronted by the unknown.

Jefferson was no intellectual reactionary. He thought that periodic revolutions keep government honest, said that given the choice between government and newspapers, he would do without the government, and was a scientist in his own right. But even he ignored the facts when they conflicted with his own conceptual framework about what is real and possible and what isn't.

Jefferson's case is not unique. For a decade, physicists ignored indications in their experiments of the positron, an atomic particle exactly like the electron except that it has a positive rather than a negative charge, simply because it was assumed that a positive charge must be carried by heavier particles, such as the proton. Similarly, chemists did not confirm that gases such as neon and argon could combine until 1962, although if any of them had taken the three or four hours necessary to check, he would have confirmed that an experiment reported twenty-three years before was valid.

According to the scientific historian T. S. Kuhn, ten or even twenty-three years is not too long to crack a preconception of the scientific community. Important concepts, such as the belief that the earth is at the center of the universe or that disease is caused by "humors" in the air rather than microbes, lasted centuries and faded only when their last stubborn supporters were dead and buried. Scientists hate to be wrong as much as anyone else.

The prevailing concept defines what research is acceptable and what isn't, which laboratories will enjoy the patronage of the pope in Galileo's time or the government today, who is published and who isn't. Parapsychology, for the most part, is an "isn't." The first American parapsychology group, the Parapsychology Association (PA) was affiliated with the American Association for the Advancement of Science in 1968, but only after a bitter debate over whether or not "affiliation" meant "recognition." Despite such gains, parapsychology remains outside the prevailing concept, a heresy to much of the scientific establishment. The affiliation of the PA with the American Association for the Advancement of Science was not followed by the universal acceptance of parapsychology in college curricula. The psychology department at the University of California at Davis, for example, offers no courses in parapsychology. Steve Glickman, chairman of the department, doesn't expect any in the future: "There is a certain rejection of things unknown."

"There have been a lot of difficulties," says consciousness researcher Charles Tart. "The vast majority of the faculty members don't know anything about parapsychology in the first place. It is a threat to their conventional belief systems." Skeptical faculty members have even moved to deny Tart tenure.

Publication of parapsychology papers in the major scientific journals is rare. The February 1982 issue of the *Proceedings of the Institute of Electrical and Electronic Engineers* included a paper by Robert Jahn, dean of Princeton University's prestigious school of engineering, surveying the current psychic research from an engineer's perspective. Jahn's paper came sixteen years after the only other paper on parapsychology ever printed by the *Proceedings*, a 1967 study of "A Perceptual Channel for Information Transfer Over Kilometer Distances," in which Stanford Research Institute physicists Harold Puthoff and Russell Targ claimed that trained psychics could "remotely view" distant geographic sites, including the surface of the planet Mercury! "That [earlier] paper was received with great interest, considerable skepticism, some hostility, and even a bit of shock," the *Proceedings'* editors warned in an introduction to Jahn's paper, but "the persistent, fragmentary indication of the possible existence of psychic phenomena requires us, in the interests of scientific integrity and intellectual honesty, to apply the same spirit of objective inquiry that we have focused on the more traditional and accepted branches of science and technology."

Few scientific journals are willing to apply the spirit of objective inquiry to articles on parapsychology. The influential British journal *Nature* published Puthoff and Targ's research on remote viewing in 1974, but it was accompanied by an editorial explaining that they had done so only to give readers a "representative" sample of the poor scientific papers submitted by parapsychologists.

Despite such official hostility, there is growing interest in parapsychology among the rank and file of the scientific community. "The physical scientists, physicists and engineers, are coming around first," says Puthoff, himself a recognized authority on the physics of lasers, "and the psychologists and journal editors last." Such interests are not without risk, as Princeton's engineering dean Robert Jahn related in the introduction to his *Proceedings* article:

I confess that I [discuss parapsychology research] with some trepidation, borne of previous unpleasant experiences. For example, a lighthearted article in the Princeton alumni magazine, in which I attempted to share some of [my] experiences in this field with the university community at large, brought an intensity and breadth of reactions for which I was totally unprepared, ranging from irresponsible and categorical condemnation on one extreme, to equally irrational messianic accolades on the other. Rather than precipitating further such distracting outbursts, I have largely avoided opportunities for public presentation.

Rank-and-file fascination with psychic phenomena runs high in the medical community too, although that interest is also unreflected in the curricula of medical schools. Stanley R. Dean, the current president of the American Society for Social Psychiatry, surveyed the faculties and found "an unprecedented degree of contemporary interest among physicians and the general public" in the forbidden subjects, including altered states of consciousness, meditation, postmortem survival, voodoo, placebo effects, and, above all, "the scientific modus operandi of so-called miraculous healing." Dean lumps them all into the term *metapsychiatry*, which he defines as "the confluence of psychiatry and psychic phenomena."[1]

Dean's survey found that 58 percent of the medical faculty polled felt that "an understanding of psychic phenomena is important to future graduates of psychiatry programs," compared to 22 percent who thought it unimportant, and that more than half wanted more research in the field. Thirty percent thought that a psychic aptitude test would be a useful diagnostic tool, and only 15 percent denied the existence of psychic phenomena. Twenty-one percent believed that all people possess some degree of psychic ability.

An even higher percentage of the American public accept the reality of psychic phenomena. Fifty-one percent believe in ESP, according to a recent Gallup poll; 37 percent also believe in precognition (the ability to see the future), and 29 percent in astrology. The United States supports twenty thousand professional astrologers and only two thousand astronomers.

Just what is parapsychology? Nonsense and superstition, as claimed by the skeptics, or a new scientific vista, or the pop-technology of the media?

Princeton's Robert Jahn compared the world of psychic research to a "fog-shrouded swamp,"

> wherein are reported to dwell a bewildering array of bizarre phenomenological creatures, all foreign to our normal perceptual and analytical catalogues. Some scholars who have explored this clouded domain have returned to announce categorically that all such life is illusionary—mere sunken stumps and swirling subsurface shadows, inviting misperception by the gullible and misrepresentation by the purveyors. But others of comparable conviction have described in minute detail their observations of a variety of extraordinary beings of awesome dimensions and capability.[2]

Man's preoccupation with strange creatures lurking in the subconscious is as old as history, first appearing in cave drawings from approximately 20,000 B.C. From the beginning, military and political leaders have sought to put these strange powers to practical use.

Sometimes the results were unfortunate, most notably for King Croesus of Lydia in ancient Greece, who sought the advice of an oracle to decide whether or not to cross the Halys River and attack the Persians. He had many to choose from, including fakers and lunatics of all description as well as established psychics such as the oracle at Delphi. The Delphic oracle was widely consulted on important matters of state and received her inspiration after breathing volcanic fumes, then thought to be the odors of corruption from a snake demon slain by Hercules. Croesus devised a test, which only the Delphic oracle answered correctly: "Croesus is boiling a lamb and a tortoise together, in a copper vessel with a copper lid." The oracle told Croesus that war with the Persians would "destroy a great empire," which the king interpreted to mean the Persian empire. In fact, the attack was a disaster; his own empire fell.

Failure more often doomed the practitioner of the arcane arts

than the sovereign patron. Alchemists who aroused expectations
of coffers full of gold ended roasted alive in iron chairs or hanged
from gilded gallows, but not all the oracles, alchemists, and magicians of old were unsuccessful. At least one became immortal—
the fame of the English alchemist, psychic, and spy 007 lives
· today.

The real, historical 007 was John Dee, an alchemist and astrologer in the court of Queen Elizabeth during the late sixteenth
century. Men's eyes fascinated Elizabeth, and her favored servants signed letters to the queen with symbolic eyes. Dee, who
headed the British espionage network, signed himself

$$\overline{0\ 0/}$$

each *0* representing an eye and the *7* the sum of two eyes, four
other senses, and last, mystical knowledge from "the nine," spirits
who spoke through Dee's crystal ball, the "shew stone." Dee
credited the nine and his shew stone with uncovering a Spanish
plot to burn the forests that provided wood for English shipbuild-
ing. Whatever the source, the plot was real. Had it succeeded, the
Spanish Armada might have sailed unopposed.

Christian writers and philosophers recount many instances of
psychic phenomena, usually attributed to visitations of divine or
demonic beings. In the view of these writers, such miracles proved
the existence of God; psychic phenomena required ideological
and political importance.

In the sixteenth century, the Swiss physician and alchemist
Paracelsus wrote:

> The mind of man is the microcosmic counterpart of the universal
> mind. . . . One man may communicate his thoughts to another with
> whom he is in sympathy, at any distance however great it may be,
> or he may act upon the spirit of another person in such a manner
> as to influence his actions.[3]

In the mid-eighteenth century, the Roman Catholic church authorized Prospero Lambertini, who later became Pope Benedict XIV, to investigate psychic phenomena. His conclusions were startlingly contemporary, namely that (1) psychic experiences are not necessarily the work of divine or demonic entities, but can affect "fools, idiots, melancholy persons, and brute beasts"; (2) prophecy occurs more often in sleep than in waking and is often symbolic; and (3) it is difficult for a prophet to distinguish his own thoughts from psychic messages.

In 1858, Charles Darwin published the *Origin of Species*. The theory of evolution's challenge to mystical and religious interpretations of the world happened to coincide with the rise of spiritualism, attempts to communicate with the dead, and that coincidence gave rise to the first scientific studies of psychic phenomena. In 1848, two sisters, Margaretta and Catherine Fox, had reported "rappings" in their parents' house in Hydesville, New York, which the sisters attributed to spirits. Séances became the rage, even in the White House, where Mary Todd Lincoln, the president's wife, unsuccessfully attempted to contact her own late parents. Persons in hypnotic trances, which resemble those of the medium, were also widely reported to perform amazing feats.

The materialists and evolutionists of the nineteenth century naturally tried to prove that such phenomena could be explained in scientific rather than divine terms. The word *parapsychology* literally means "beside psychology" and was coined by German psychologist and occult investigator Max Dessoir in the 1880s, about the time those first scientific studies of spiritualism, hypnotism, and psychic phenomena began. The Society for Psychical Research was founded in London in 1882, and an American society began three years later.

Today, words like *spiritualism* are anathema to serious parapsychology researchers. Parapsychology has achieved a degree of independence from those scientifically disreputable antecedents. Although many discourage the study of parapsychology, at least twenty U.S. universities do support research programs in parapsychology, and one, John F. Kennedy University in Orinda, California, offers a master's program. There are at least eight English-language journals devoted to the scholarly study of parapsychology.

The John F. Kennedy University master's program defines parapsychology as "the scientific study of psi phenomena, that is, apparent exchanges between living beings and the world around them that do not seem explainable by the known laws of the physical universe."

Psi is the term used by parapsychologists to describe the whole range of phenomena under study. Speaking broadly, there are two major kinds of psi, or psychic phenomena: extrasensory perception, or ESP, and psychokinesis, or PK. Psychokinesis means "psychic kinetics," or mind over matter, the ability to move or influence objects without the application of any known physical force. Uri Geller made PK famous by bending spoons and keys, apparently by force of mind.

ESP is less well defined, and researchers often speak of GESP, or "general ESP," rather than specifically telepathy (mind-to-mind communication), clairvoyance (the ability to perceive hidden objects), precognition (knowing the future), or "out-of-body experiences," OOBE.

Parapsychologists do not always agree on just how broadly general ESP or psi should be defined. A bewildering variety of anomalous phenomena—reported events incongruous with the commonly accepted norms of science—have been labeled parapsychological by one researcher or another: poltergeists (mischievous ghosts), astrology, cryptozoology (the study of alleged beasts such as Bigfoot, the Abominable Snowman, and the Loch Ness monster), mysterious castrations of farm animals in the Midwest, faith healing, transcendental meditation, Tibetan weather patterns (allegedly controlled psychokinetically by monks), and UFOs. According to Jeffrey Mishlove, the first person to receive a Ph.D. in parapsychology from a major U.S. university (U. of

California at Berkeley), there is a schism between those parapsychologists who would restrict the study to the less controversial
phenomena and those, like himself, who would adopt a subjective
approach and "extend the self-conscious, critical history of parapsychology further into the prescientific cultural traditions of sha-
manism, yoga, Sufism, and kabbalah."

Most parapsychologists would probably include poltergeists
among the legitimate interests of their field, although no one
uses that word. RSPK, "remote spontaneous psychokinetic
phenomena," smacks less of the occult than mischievous ghost.
Poltergeists are among the best studied of laboratory phenomena.
They manifest themselves in homes for a few weeks or months,
breaking glasses and opening windows and doors in the middle of
the night, and then disappear. Invariably, a disturbed teenager
lives in the affected house, and parapsychologists theorize that
RSPK phenomena may be psychic manifestations of the child's
turmoil.

Most parapsychologists would probably exclude astrology from
the field, although one of the most controversial and apparently
successful recent studies in the anomalous sciences purports to
show a correlation between success in sports and the position of
Mars at birth. The "Mars effect" study, published in European
scientific journals in 1980 by Michel and Francoise Gauquelin,
has so far withstood every attack outraged critics could muster.
Until someone does a contrary study or finds fault in the Gauque-
lins' work, the anomaly stands.

My guess is that parapsychologists would split evenly on UFOs.
Certainly persons interested in parapsychology are often also interested in UFOs; for example, personnel assigned to the photography section of the Office of Naval Intelligence, which participated in much of the military research in psychic weapons, also
studied UFOs, both officially and avocationally. A number of
prominent UFOlogists theorize that UFOs are psychic rather
than extraterrestrial in origin. A number of prominent psychics,

including Uri Geller, trace the origin of their powers to extraterrestrials in the UFOs. Some deny any connection between UFOs and ESP, no matter how generally defined, or just aren't interested in one or the other.

Much of the current research on general ESP involves out-of-body experiences, especially remote viewing, or the ability to leave one's physical body and visit distant geographic sites. While the terminology has been modernized, the alchemist Paracelsus described the phenomenon four hundred years ago:

> Man also possesses a power by which he may see his friends and the circumstances by which they are surrounded, although such persons may be a thousand miles away from him at the time.

Remote-viewing experiments use one of two experimental procedures, both developed by Harold Puthoff and Russel Targ at Stanford Research Institute. One procedure is to give the psychic subject simple geographic coordinates, such as a latitude and a longitude; the psychic then describes the site. Alternately, the researchers may actually visit the target site. The psychic, usually isolated so that he cannot possibly communicate with the people at the site, then describes or draws his impressions.

Puthoff and Targ report that "apparently everyone can experience remote viewing."[4] With practice, the average person performs as well as the professional psychic; the results of inexperienced subjects "are simply less reliable" than those of the pro.[5]

The "more reliable" results Puthoff and Targ report with talented subjects seem reliable indeed. One subject described the exact contents of a locked file cabinet three thousand miles away. An even longer range remote viewing showed that the planet Jupiter had faint rings like those of its neighbor Saturn. Astronomers scoffed at this claim; Carl Sagan called it "ridiculous." Nine years later, *Voyager 1* sent back pictures of the Jovian rings.

"It is generally believed that the Soviets and their allies are well in the lead in parapsychology research," Lieutenant Colonel Alexander asserts in his *Military Review* article on the psychic battlefield. "This belief is supported by a number of popular books that have been on the market for the past ten years." According to Alexander, parapsychology defies the prevailing concepts of the American scientific establishment and therefore receives little funding or encouragement; Soviet researchers, in contrast, accept "the reality of paranormal events . . . and theories have been developed to explain and study those events. The Soviets have further developed techniques to control and actively employ their knowledge of parapsychology."

Alexander cites intelligence reports prepared by the Defense Intelligence Agency and the Office of the Surgeon General to support his contention that American skepticism has given the Soviets a head start in a psychic arms race. According to one such report, Soviet research in parapsychology

> is significant because of the energy and resources being allotted for this work in the Soviet Union and because of its military implications, especially in mind manipulation . . . . The more sinister aspects of paranormal research appear to be surfacing in the Soviet Union. Why else would Soviet researchers make the statement: "Tell America the psychic potential of man must be used for good."

Even the major American media have been quick to accept Alexander's assumption. "NBC Magazine" concluded a major investigation of Soviet parapsychology with the assertion that "the only thing that seems certain is that the Russians at least think there is something in parapsychology."[6]

If so, it is difficult to see how Soviet parapsychologists could avoid the ideological conflicts and "occultist" images that have kept Western researchers out of the mainstream. Research in the Soviet Union must conform not only to the prevailing scientific concepts, but also to the political concepts of Marxism. Appointment of officials influential in science and education—ministers of education and argiculture, presidents of the All-Union Academy of Sciences, deans of universities—are all controlled by the Communist party. The publication of school textbooks and even the award of scientific degrees to individuals depend on ideological orthodoxy.

According to Marxist philosophy, history is determined by material reality. Supernatural, divine, or other nonmaterial interventions are fictions created by the ruling class, deluding the oppressed classes with the belief that their condition is the result of some ordained natural order rather than the greed of the ruling class. Marx called religion "the opiate of the masses."

Marxist theory defines consciousness as a reflection of the material world. Consciousness is acted upon by material reality, not the reverse. According to the official Soviet encyclopedia, mind power just doesn't exist in Marxism: "Thought can neither be seen in the modern microscope nor can it be weighed or measured by a slide rule. Consciousness does not possess physical properties."

Although Russian scientists had studied telepathy both before and after the Communist revolution, the record shows that parapsychology has been even more controversial in Soviet scientific circles than in the West. Stalin considered the idea that nonmaterial consciousness can produce physical effects like telepathy a deliberate attack on Marxist dogma. According to the party-approved encyclopedia, telepathy was "the antiscientific, idealistic fiction about supernatural abilities of man to perceive phenomena that by location and time are inaccessible to perception."

Stalin's prescription for researchers with the temerity to disagree was somewhat more drastic than the skepticism and funding constraints that bedevil American researchers; Soviet heretics were exiled to Siberia or shot. Research stopped in 1938. However few researchers there were in the United States willing to risk the ostracism of the scientific establishment to pursue psychic investigations, we can be assured that even fewer were willing to risk firing squads in the Soviet Union until well after Stalin's death in 1953.

Ironically, it was Soviet fear of an American lead in psychic weapons that reopened the door for Soviet researchers. In 1960, the French magazine *Science et Vie* reported that the the U.S. Navy had conducted successful telepathy experiments with the nuclear submarine *Nautilus*. US NAVY USES ESP ON ATOMIC SUB! the headlines screamed. "Is telepathy a new secret weapon? Will ESP be a deciding factor in future warfare? Has the American military learned the secret of mind power?"

The French report, indignantly denied by the U.S. government, went off like a depth charge in the mind of Leonid L. Vasiliev, who had continued his own research in telepathy secretly despite Stalin's ban. In April 1960, seven years after Stalin's death, he addressed a symposium of Soviet scientists:

> We carried out extensive and until now completely unreported investigations under the Stalin regime. Today the American navy is testing telepathy on their atomic submarines. Soviet scientists conducted a great many successful telepathy tests over a quarter of a century ago. It's urgent that we throw off our prejudices. We must again plunge into the exploration of this vital field. (Quoted in Ostrander and Schroeder, *Psychic Discoveries Behind the Iron Curtain*, p. 38 [1970].)

Although the French report was soon revealed as a hoax, both the popular Soviet press and some officials in the scientific community continued to trumpet the alleged *Nautilus* tests as proof of a psychic arms gap. *Biological Radio Communications*, a major study of Soviet psychic research published in 1962, even added to the *Nautilus* legend. President Eisenhower had personally approved the test, the Soviet author asserted, and both Westinghouse and the Rand Corporation assisted in the research, which received funds from the U.S. Air Force as well as the navy.

It wasn't long before the shoe was on the other foot, and stories of questionable accuracy about amazing Soviet advances in psychic research began surfacing in the American popular press. One Soviet researcher, Pavel Naumov, declared that it did not matter whether or not the *Nautilus* report was a hoax—"If your navy didn't do the *Nautilus* experiment, then Soviet scientists were the first in the world to test ESP from a submarine!"

Soviet scientists, Naumov claimed, placed baby rabbits aboard a submarine. "They kept the mother rabbit in a laboratory on shore where they implanted electrodes deep in her brain. When the sub was deep below the surface of the ocean, assistants killed the young rabbits one by one.

"The mother rabbit obviously didn't know what was happening. Even if she could have understood the test, she had no way of knowing at what moment her children died. Yet, at each synchronized instant of death, her brain reacted. There was communication," says Naumov.

One apocalyptic account of Soviet research, the popular book *Psychic Discoveries Behind the Iron Curtain,* by Sheila Ostrander and Lynn Schroeder, suggested that the Soviets had amassed an army of "two million trained psychics" to subjugate the world for the Kremlin.

The reported Soviet advances alarmed the Pentagon and some members of Congress, who demanded that the United States do whatever was necessary to close the "psycho-gap" with the Soviets. The stories also alarmed orthodox ideologues in the Soviet Union. A 1973 article entitled "Parapsychology—Fact or Fiction?" put Soviet researchers on notice that deviations from Marxist orthodoxy would not be tolerated:

In speaking about publications, one cannot fail to mention certain political speculations in parapsychology. We have in mind primarily the book of S. Ostrander and L. Schroeder *Psychic Discoveries Behind the Iron Curtain* . . . the authors (nonscientists) wrote a low-standard work of sensational value. In addition, parapsychology serves as publicity for anti-Sovietism, while the anti-Sovietism serves as publicity for the parapsychology. The entire undertaking turned out to be commercial in the highest degree, and in about two years the book ran into five editions. The book was written at a very low professional level; it abounds in factual errors, blunders, and blunt anti-Soviet attacks. In the book, the "achievements" of native parapsychologists are overexaggerated. Similar exaggerations are encountered rather frequently in the Western press, especially in the parapsychological and popular press (frequently without overt anti-Soviet accompaniment). Very often speculations are encountered on the themes parapsychology and defense, psychological war, intelligence gathering, etc. All this serves as a means for obtaining additional financing for parapsychological investigations.

When the Voice of America broadcast excerpts from *Psychic Discoveries Behind the Iron Curtain,* Soviet officials sharply curtailed foreign contact with parapsychology researchers. Naumov, who was one of the authors' primary sources, was arrested and sentenced to hard labor in Siberia. His laboratory was closed, and his associates were dismissed.

Skeptics in this country have launched their own offensive. "There is an epidemic of irrationality that needs to be stopped," according to astronomer Carl Sagan. Sagan is one of the scientific celebrities associated with the Committee for the Scientific Investigation of Claims of the Paranormal (CSICOP).

CSICOP was the brainchild of Professor Paul Kurtz of the State University of New York at Buffalo. Its purpose, says Kurtz, "is simply to combat nonsense." Besides Sagan and Kurtz, members include behaviorist B. F. Skinner, magician James Randi, philosopher Ernest Nagel, and science-fiction great Isaac Asimov.

Many parapsychologists regard CSICOP as an intellectual vigilante group, ready to hold a kangaroo court and lynching for any researcher with the temerity to claim successful psychic experimentation. Others welcome the scrutiny. In general, however, the relations between parapsychologists and skeptics more resemble guerrilla warfare than scientific dialogue; winners would gladly exile losers to Siberia if they could.

McDonnell-Douglas Aircraft has had the honor of hosting the most notorious battle. McDonnell laboratories houses air force research on psychic security for nuclear weapons, and the non-profit McDonnell foundation has generously funded private research nationwide. The largest single project, however, is the McDonnell Laboratory for Psychical Research in Saint Louis, which opened in 1979 with a five-hundred-thousand-dollar annual grant to two researchers, Peter R. Phillips and Mark Shafer.

Ostensibly, Phillips and Shafer are studying psychokinetic metal-bending (PKMB), the ability to psychically bend or distort small metal objects such as spoons and keys with little or no physical contact. The ultimate goal of the research is more ambitious—the late McDonnell hoped to contact dead test pilots. Metal-bending, he believed, can identify and train promising psychics.

McDonnell believed in the occult, which is why airplanes manufactured by his company have included the "Phantom" and the "Voodoo" fighters. He was a giant in his industry and lobbied unceasingly for increased government support of psychic research.

Former CIA director Adm. Stansfield Turner remembers McDonnell as "perceptive, forward looking, and patriotic" and is open to the possibility that McDonnell was right. "Twenty years from now, I may wonder how I could be so dumb as to question the evidence for psychic phenomena," says Turner, "but then again, I may feel the same way I do now."

McDonnell's interest in the dead was not unique. In 1920, inventor Thomas Edison told *Scientic American* magazine he had "been thinking for some time of a machine or apparatus that could be operated by personalities who have passed on to another existence or sphere. I believe that if we are to make any real progress in psychic investigation, we must do it with scientific apparatus and in a scientific manner." Officials at the Edison National Historic Site in West Orange, New Jersey, call Edison's remarks a jest, but the *Scientific American* took him seriously. Edison hoped to complete the apparatus, "in the nature of a valve" to magnify messages from the afterworld, within a few months of the interview.

Soon afterward, serious parapsychologists got out of the afterworld business. They did not want to be skewered on the same sword with which the great magician Houdini crusaded to expose the hucksters who exploited the bereaved with phony séances. For years, parapsychology researchers shunned anything that might smack of the field's beginnings in spiritualism, but currently postmortem survival is again the subject of serious study by the parapsychology community. It is still precisely the sort of thing that makes skeptics snicker about *implicit* "occult" theories, but even Robert Jahn lists "the systematic and conservative reincarnation studies at the University of Virginia" among the most convincing studies suggesting the reality of psychic phenomena. A California company, Heavens Union, sends letters postmortem, $60 for one hundred words, $200 for "priority service." Messages to hell or dead pets are not accepted. Another company offers closed-cicuit TV to heaven. Sales have been brisk.

The Central Intelligence Agency has been interested too. During the fifties, according to former agent Victor Marchetti, the agency tried to contact dead Soviet agents in the hope that in an afterthought from their graves, they would realize the error of Communist materialism and defect to the West.

Phillips and Shafer are by nature more cautious and have not attempted to contact the dead. They have reported successful metal-bending by two male subjects, "M.E." and "S.S." (their real names are Michael Edwards and Steve Shaw). Both men are in their early twenties and responded to advertisements placed in newspapers across the country when the McDonnell Laboratory for Psychical Research opened in 1979. They claim the ability to

bend small metal objects such as spoons and keys by gently stroking them with their fingers while concentrating psychic force, in
the same manner as Israeli psychic Uri Geller.

Phillips and Shafer claimed to have tested their subjects' abilities under rigorous scientific controls, including video tapes to
detect and record any attempted cheating. The video tapes were
shown at the August 1981 convention of the Parapsychological
Association.

In their briefing for the convention, Phillips and Shafer defined
the goals of their research as "exploring the range of their [M.E.
and S.S.] ability, discovering what conditions seem to be condu-
cive for its occurrence, obtaining well-controlled evidence for
macro-PK (metal-bending), and obtaining convincing video records" of metal-bending.

Both subjects claim success in metal-bending for many years,
one using a visualization technique from the martial arts and the
other by "ridding his mind of all thought so that his subconscious
can go to work." The subjects, said Phillips and Shafer, "proved
very open to our experimental requirements, although they claim
to feel uneasy around electronic equipment."

The video tapes were not well received by the Parapsychology
Association. A few suspected that M.E. and S.S. were magicians
planted by James Randi, a well-known magician, escape artist,
and hatchet man for CSICOP. Others felt Randi and the researchers might be in collusion to embarrass the convention by
getting its endorsement for the video tapes.

Phillips and Shafer, confronted by the skeptics, insisted that
their laboratory procedures precluded successful cheating. The
McDonnell foundation kept faith with its researchers and even
convinced the Hoffman-LaRoche drug company that the psychics might be able to perform genetic engineering more cheaply
than conventional techniques for gene transplants.

Unfortunately for Phillips and Shafer, the suspicious members
of the Parapsychology Association were right. In March 1983,

Randi revealed the hoax on the front pages of the newspapers all over the world. Phillips and Shafer finally had to admit they had been had.

Throughout it all, Randi faithfully acted as an "adviser" to Phillips and Shafer and correctly informed them how the subjects' tricks were done and how cheating can be prevented. He even went so far as to denounce M.E. and S.S. as frauds in an open letter to the PA, but not openly admitting that he knew them.

"First McDonnell and then, I hope, the other so-called prestigious parapsychology laboratories will endorse M.E. and S.S. as genuine," Randi boasted before revealing his hoax, thus "discrediting parapsychology research all over the world."

Actually, the results of the hoax were more ambiguous. Randi sprang his trap early so he could use it for the premiere of his own TV show, so early, in fact, that Phillips and Shafer had not officially published their experiments. Despite their statements to the Parapsychological Association, by scientific protocol a researcher has claimed nothing until he publishes. By that standard, Randi didn't catch Phillips and Shafer or anyone else. Serious questions were raised about the ethics of the hoax, although even Phillips called it "worthwhile." Among other things, Randi's ringers ingratiated themselves to the McDonnell staff by suggesting they might use their powers to cure one researcher's daughter, who suffered from serious eye problems.

As Phillips and Shafer learned to their sorrow, magicians have dozens of techniques for bending metal. Uri Geller sometimes uses a small vise hidden in his belt buckle—the audience's attention is misdirected, the key bent, and the bent portion covered with his hand. Geller then gradually uncovers the already bent key as he rubs it, creating the illusion that the gentle stroking causes rather than uncovers the bend.

Magicians keep such sophisticated techniques secret, but even very simple deceptions can be effective. One Sunday I told a waitress at my favorite Mexican restaurant that I, too, was a novice psychic metal-bender. I asked the waitress to get two identical forks, one for me to bend and the other for comparison: "I'm not a very experienced psychic, so it's sometimes hard to see the bend."

With some trepidation, since I expected to be denounced as a charlatan and tarred with bean dip, I asked the waitress to choose the fork I was to bend, hold it in her hand, close her eyes, and think "up." She closed her eyes; I pressed the comparison fork against the table and bent it down. When the two forks were compared, the one she held was "up" in comparison to the "normal" spoon I had bent down.

She swallowed the trick, but don't think the waitress was uniquely naïve. Uri Geller fooled the national science correspondent for *Time* magazine, John Wilhelm, with the same trick.

Belief in phony psychic phenomena is easy to form and hard to shake. Perhaps the best demonstration of the willingness of even well-educated, inquiring people to swallow psychic grandstanding was reported in 1980 by psychologists Barry Singer and Victor A. Benassi of the California State University at Long Beach in an article entitled "Fooling Some of the People All of the Time."[7] Singer and Benassi introduced a performer, Craig Reynolds, to four of their classes. Two of the classes were told that Reynolds, dressed in a purple choir robe, sandals, and a starburst medallion, was a "graduate student interested in the psychology of the paranormal or psychic abilities." The instructors warned that they "were not convinced personally" of Reynolds's or anyone else's psychic abilities. In two other classes, Reynolds was introduced as a magician, and the students were advised that all of the feats Reynolds would perform were "easy amateur tricks that have been practiced for centuries and are even explained in children's books of magic."

In each class, Reynolds read ten three-digit numbers while blindfolded, smeared cigarette ashes on the backs of a student's hands and then transferred them to her palms, and finally bent a steel rod by gently stroking it with his fingers while the students chanted "bending."

The results of the experiment were disconcerting to anyone planning to attend the University of California. Not only did three quarters of the students in classes where Reynolds was introduced as a psychic swallow the act, two thirds of the students in the classes where he was introduced as a magician were nevertheless convinced he was really a psychic. Students covered their papers with talisman symbols as protection against the devil and chanted exorcisms. Eighteen percent reported "fright and emotional disturbance."

Singer and Benassi were present at two of the Reynolds performances. Halfway through the bending chant, they reported, "the class was in a terribly excited state. Students sat rigidly in their chairs, eyes glazed and mouths open, chanting together. When the rod bent, they gasped and murmured. After class was dismissed, they typically sat still in their chairs, staring vacantly or shaking their heads, or rushed excitedly up to Craig [Reynolds], asking him how they could develop such powers."

Singer and Benassi call the results of their experiment "bizarre" and suggest that "people can stubbornly maintain a belief about someone's psychic powers when they know better. . . . Are we humans really that foolish? Yes."

To a certain extent, the Pentagon stands above the sniping between the parapsychologists and the skeptics. The Pentagon has the statutory responsibility to investigate all new technologies, if only to ensure that the other side doesn't surprise us. Few thought the atomic bomb would work; even the scientists who built it vied for the low numbers in an office pool on the yield of the first test.

Parapsychology allegedly played an important role in World War II. The stories of psychic victories during the war, and the captured records of Nazi parapsychology experiments in the concentration camps, intrigued U.S. researchers, who thought the

Germans might have been close to discovering practical psychic weapons.

Many of the war stories proved false, including the feats attributed to Peter Hurkos, the "Radar Brain Man" later hired by the Bridgewater, New Jersey, police. The World War II claims of Hurkos and his authorized biographers were exhaustively checked by Dutch journalist Piet Hein Hoebens, with the assistance of the Dutch State Institute for War Documentation, the most complete archives of its kind.[8]

Hurkos supposedly acquired his uncanny gifts after a fall from a ladder in 1941, while Holland was occupied by the Nazis. In his autobiography, he claims to have joined an underground group led by "a man named Hert Goozens, one of the bravest men in the entire system of secret fighters."

By his own account, Hurkos's most daring feat was the rescue of Yap Mindemon, a Dutch resistance fighter who had been arrested by the Germans and taken to a camp in the town of Vught. Hurkos stole a German officer's uniform and presented himself as "Wehrmachtkapitan Robert Fischner." "In flawless German," he informed the camp commandant that Mindemon was wanted at headquarters for questioning. The Germans readily believed him and took him to the cell where his friend was held.

As Hurkos entered the barracks, he psychically sensed that Mindemon believed he had gone over to the Germans. "In a moment, I could feel, he would shout and denounce me to the Germans." Hurkos had no choice. Cursing, he kicked and beat Mindemon unconscious and then drove him to safety in the car thoughtfully loaned to "Wehrmachtkapitan Fischner" by the commandant.

After the occupation ended, the legend says, Hurkos was decorated by Queen Wilhelmina for his "valorous deeds in the service of the fatherland."

That's what the legend says, but the war archives contain "no information on any underground activities by Mr. Hurkos" and no mention at all of a man named Hert Goozens, allegedly leader of the underground group. The queen never decorated Hurkos, and the records of the prisoner camp at Vught do not mention the alleged rescue of Mindemon. "The story seems to be a product of the imagination," Dutch researchers concluded. Nevertheless, Hurkos's wartime heroics are recounted in at least two biographies published in English, and dozens of other books and magazines discuss the Vught rescue as an established fact. To the casual researcher, especially one who does not speak Dutch and doesn't have access to the war archives, the psychic rescue of Yap Mindemon might appear indisputably well documented.

Some of the Nazis themselves might have had good reason to believe the Hurkos tale, the records notwithstanding. The incredible successes of British intelligence, some high-ranking Germans concluded, could only be attributed to telepathy or clairvoyance; few would have believed the truth—the Allies had decoded the "unbreakable" German and Japanese codes—even if the suspicion had been raised.

The British deliberately fostered the mystical image of their intelligence services. Agent Ian Fleming, who later created James Bond in the image of Queen Elizabeth's 007, John Dee, used doctored horoscopes to convince Hitler's second-in-command, Rudolf Hess, that the stars favored a secret peace initiative on May 10, 1941. Hess parachuted into Scotland and British captivity.

Not all the Allied interest in parapsychology was spurious. Psychic Edgar I. Cayce advised Gen. John Pershing and accompanied him on European missions. Gen. George Patton used a water dowser in North Africa. When his dowser protested that a suitable willow tree could not be found for the rod, Patton flew in a sapling from Georgia.

Most of the myths about psychic superweapons developed in World War II started with the private interest of an individual who happened to be in the military, particularly, as in these cases, when that individual was either high ranking or attached to a secretive branch of the service.

The notorious "Philadelphia experiments" are typical of the mythology. In 1956, author Morris K. Jessup sent a copy of his newly published book, *The Case for the UFO,* to the Office for Naval Research, along with letters he had received from one Carlos Allende. Allende claimed UFOs were manifestations of a superweapon based on Einstein's unified field theory and first tested at the Philadelphia navy yard. According to Allende, the navy teleported the destroyer S.S. *Andrew Furnseth* from its dock to the Newport News yard and back again, all in five minutes. Half the crew was lost, and the rest, including Allende, suffered bizarre effects. Some went as "mad as hatters," others froze in position or blinked in and out. Two men touched, and "possibly because of the metal on one of them," they began to smolder. "Both men burned for eighteen days," claimed Allende.

The book intrigued several persons in the office, who, wholly at their own expense, reproduced several copies of the book and mailed an annotated copy back to Jessup. Ever since, dozens of magazine articles and books have insisted the navy's interest must have been official. Even Allende's confession that the letters were a hoax did not dampen the enthusiasm of the secret-weapon buffs. Allende, they insist, was silenced by the navy, and Jessup, who died in 1959, an apparent suicide, was murdered because he knew too much.

During the war, there was considerable concern that the Nazis had developed a UFO-like secret weapon, possibly based on their psychic and occult studies. In the final months of the war, when the Germans introduced the first jet fighter and the first guided antiaircraft missiles, small balls of light began to appear around Allied aircraft. The lights, dubbed "foo fighters" or "kraut balls," varied from the size of golf balls to beach balls and glowed or blinked red, white, or gold. No one has ever explained the mystery of the foo fighters, but they are one of the best documented UFO phenomena, reported and sometimes photographed by hundreds of pilots. The foo fighters disappeared when the Allies crossed the

Rhine, reportedly because the secret Nazi laboratories had to close.

The Nazis made good use of their own phony psychics. Eric Jan Hannussen, a flamboyant stage performer and psychic consultant on everything from personal finance to astrology, billed himself the "Prophet of the Third Reich." Hannussen published a popular astrological magazine, *Hannusens Bunte Wochenshau* ("Colorful Weekly Forecast"), which emphasized the "historical inevitability" of Nazi triumph, and ingratiated himself personally to Nazi bigwigs with generous loans. In 1931, Hannussen's friends arranged an audience with Hitler, who promised to establish an "Academy of the Occult" headed by Hannussen. The prophet, however, was destined to survive only two months of the promised Thousand-Year Reich.

On February 26, 1933, Hannussen gave a lavish reception at his recently opened "Palace of the Occult," a showplace of golden zodiacs, hothouses teeming with exotic plants, venomous snakes and salamanders, centrally controlled lighting effects and hidden microphones with which Hannussen could eavesdrop on his powerful guests. At exactly midnight, the lights went dark and the "Prophet of the Third Reich" appeared in a glowing circle of glass. His eyes hidden by a black mask and his voice filled with foreboding, Hannussen warned that Hitler's "magnificent victory" in the coming elections might be threatened:

"I see flames, enormous flames. . . . It is a terrible conflagration that has broken out. Criminals have set a fire.

They want to hurl Germany into last-minute chaos, to nullify the victory. They are setting fire to a large public building. One must crush this vermin. They want to resist Hitler's victory. Only the mailed fist of an awakened Germany can hold back chaos and the threat of civil war. . . ."

At nine-thirty the next morning, the Reichstag burned, giving the Nazis their excuse to cancel elections they were expected to lose.

Two months later, Hannussen overplayed his hand, trying to collect some of his personal loans from important Nazis, and was arrested for "inveigling into the National Socialist [Nazi] party through the use of forged papers." Ten days later, his decomposed body was found in a wooded area outside Berlin, the victim, according to the police, of "underworld elements" with whom Hannussen had recently begun to associate.

Hitler himself, by many accounts, believed in the occult, although the best Hitler scholars emphatically dissent. Nevertheless, the Führer may have been genuinely impressed by Hannussen, who was a talented magician. Not every Nazi, however, believed in the occult. Goebbels used psychics and astrologers for propaganda, but was himself a skeptic and personally hated Hannussen.

Goebbel's skepticism aside, not all the Nazi research into parapsychology and the occult was spurious. The notorious "aviation experiments" at Dachau concentration camp included tests to determine whether telepathy increased under torture, as well as tests in which Jews and Gypsies were frozen to death in vats of ice water to determine how long downed pilots could survive in the icy English Channel.

There is no doubt that captured records of these experiments interested U.S. intelligence, and American researchers assumed the Soviets took the same interest (to this day, some claim the Soviets still experiment with the effect of torture on telepathy). Korean War reports that American prisoners had succumbed to Communist "brainwashing" exacerbated these suspicions, and organized U.S. investigation of "the things the Nazis undertook to do"[9] began at the CIA's technical services division in 1952. Nazi rocket research had revolutionized warfare; the agency, responsible men concluded, had a statutory and moral responsibility to ensure that the Soviets were not the sole benefactor of the Dachau experiments, no matter how repugnant. The records of those experiments are still classified top secret.

NOTES

1. Dean, Stanley R. *Journal of American Society for Social Psychiatry,* October 1981.
2. Jahn, Robert. *Proceedings of the IEEE,* February 1982.
3. Hartmann, F. *Paracelsus: Life and Prophecies,* 1973.
4. Puthoff and Targ, *Mind Reach,* 1977, p. 4.
5. Ibid., p. 10.
6. *NBC Magazine,* March 13, 1981.
7. *Skeptical Enquirer,* October 1980.
8. *Zetetic Scholar,* Spring 1982.
9. Quoted from documents released by the C.I.A. in 1982 under the Freedom of Information Act.

3·PSYCHIC ARMS RACE?

IF the United States loses a psychic arms race with the Soviets, no one will blame Congressman Charlie Rose. "The Russians are up to their [hip pocket]* in this stuff," he says. "We shouldn't fall behind."

Rose should know. Not only does he sit on the House Select Committee on Intelligence, but he has investigated psychic weapons himself.

Congressman Rose fits the southern image; he is a devout Presbyterian, a former county prosecutor, and champion of the tobacco lobby. He is also the House's acknowledged expert on computers and founder of the Congressional Clearinghouse on the Future, an informal caucus financed by private contributions.

Rose founded the Clearinghouse after futurist Alvin Toffler, author of *Future Shock*, convinced him that Congress needed to consider the impact of future technology in its legislation. Today the Clearinghouse newsletter publishes articles on space colonies, gene manipulation, "soft" energy, and other New Age issues.

At present, Rose doesn't think the United States needs to spend a lot of money on psychic weapons, but only because "we just don't know how to build them." When the needed technological breakthroughs come, he says, we may need a "psychic Manhattan Project."

The congressman's personal experience has convinced him

*The original expletive has been deleted, at Rose's request.

such breakthroughs are on the horizon. He has attended classified demonstrations of remote viewing arranged by the CIA. Says Rose, "I've seen some incredible examples of remote viewing— so much so that I think we ought to pay close attention to developments in this field, and especially to what the Soviets are doing. If they develop a capacity to have people mentally view secret centers within this country, we could come to the point where we didn't have any secrets."

Rose thinks skeptics in the Pentagon and CIA are hindering U.S. research in remote viewing and wonders openly about their motives. "We may have to investigate them," he warns.

"Some of the intelligence people I've talked to know that remote viewing works, although they still block further research on it, since they claim it's not yet as accurate as satellite photography," according to Rose. "But it seems to me that it would be a hell of a cheap radar system, and if the Russians have it and we don't, we are in serious trouble. This country wasn't afraid to look into the strange physics behind lasers and semiconductors, and I don't think it should be afraid to look at this."

Rose is personally not afraid to look into the subject; he has even tested prototype psychic weapons. Once he allowed a test on himself, and once on an unknowing House Speaker Thomas ("Tip") O'Neill.

Early in 1981, a group of investors asked the congressman's help in securing Pentagon funding for an electronic paranoia inducer. Astronics, Inc., hoped to manufacture the "psychic neuron disrupter," which, according to the inventors, interferes with the connections between nerve cells in the brain and induces temporary paranoia. The physiological effect, they say, is "similar to that of hallucinogenic drugs such as LSD, but transmitted electronically." The range of the existing device is supposedly limited, but could be extended for military applications. Rose submitted himself to a test of the machine, and he thinks it worked: "We don't know how to build the hyperspatial nuclear howitzer, but we do know how to jam the synaptic connections of the nervous system. It deserves some research money." Despite weeks of negotiations and apparent interest at the Pentagon, no contract was signed. The company folded a year later.

Rose also tested telepathic hypnosis with the help of Judith Skutch, a wealthy New York patron of psychic research who teaches "A Course in Miracles" at the Army War College. With Rose standing at her side, Skutch and several other psychics associated with the Army War College broadcast psychic "love emanations" at Speaker O'Neill from the gallery of the House, commanding the unknowing majority leader to turn his head left and right on command, and then, according to one participant, commanding him to favor public works projects in the congressman's district. Skutch claims the same can be done to the Soviet leadership, and Barbara Marx Hubbard, a noted psychologist whom the army consults on psychic developments, hopes to "bombard the Kremlin with love, not missiles." Rose refuses to comment on the incident.

Rose's concern over a putative "psycho-gap" with the Soviet Union is shared, albeit more discreetly, by many congressmen. The 1970 publication of the popular and luridly sensational *Psychic Discoveries Behind the Iron Curtain*[1] by Sheila Ostrander and Lynn Schroeder generated strong congressional pressure on the Defense Department to fund its own psychic research. Congressman Claude Pepper (D-Fla) declared that this "remarkable" and "impressively annotated" book described "astounding technological findings," to which "our country will not be indifferent."[2] Astounding indeed was the book's revelation that Soviet "witch covens" had warned British colleagues that the Soviets were amassing an army of two million trained psychics to subjugate the world. Rose still maintains the Soviets "have a national screening program to detect mathematical, artistic, or psychic ability in schoolchildren."

Psychic Discoveries Behind the Iron Curtain also suggested a connection between Soviet parapsychology research and UFOs, raising the possibility of a UFO race in addition to the psychic arms race: "It isn't coincidental that parapsychologists, astrophysicists, and UFOlogists blend at Moscow seminars."

Dr. J. Allen Hynek, chairman of the astronomy department at Northwestern University and one of the leading American UFOlogists, wrote in *Playboy* magazine that his greatest fear was that he would someday unfold his paper to read "Russians Solve UFO Mystery." The Soviets train astronauts in ESP, possibly to contact extraterrestrials, a feat that Hynek justifiably said would "shake America so hard that the launching of *Sputnik* in 1957 would appear in retrospect as important as a Russian announcement of a particularly large wheat crop."

Even more astounding, however, were the conclusions of a 1972 Defense Intelligence Agency (DIA) study, originally classified top secret but released in 1978. "Soviet efforts in the field of [psychic] research," the agency predicted, sooner or later might enable them to do some of the following:

A. Know the contents of top secret U.S. documents, the deployment of our troops and ships, and the location and nature of our military installations.
B. Mold the thoughts of key U.S. military and civilian leaders, at a distance.
C. Cause the instant death of any U.S. official, at a distance.
D. Disable, at a distance, U.S. military equipment of all types, including spacecraft.[3]

These apocalyptic predictions, incredible as they seem, have echoed repeatedly in intelligence evaluations to the present day. According to a 1975 DIA study,[4] also released in 1978, Soviet psychotronic weapons "would pose a severe threat to enemy military, embassy, or security functions."

A still-classified 1975 CIA estimate warns that the "Soviets possibly lead the U.S. in applied parapsychology studies." The analysts estimated that "the Soviet military and KGB have had a covert applied parapsychology program since the mid-1960s" and noted that "several independent U.S. laboratories recently have demonstrated the existence of paranormal phenomena. Such phenomena may have intelligence applications."

In 1976, the CIA contracted for an exhaustive review of Soviet parapsychology research by outside experts.[5] One of the physicists who helped write the report, Dr. J. W. Eerkens, now believes "the Soviets are actually building prototype equipment for psychic warfare."

The most sensational claims of Soviet psychic secrets come from retired army Lt. Col. Thomas Bearden, formerly an army intelligence analyst. Bearden says the Soviets have psychic hyperspatial nuclear howitzers that "could denude the strategic capability of the free world with a single shot"[6] by transmitting a single nuclear explosion instantaneously to a limitless number of sites anywhere in the universe. Rose calls the concept "really something."

Lt. Col. John Alexander's article in the *Military Review* notes that "the use of telepathic hypnosis also holds great potential. This capability could allow agents to be deeply planted with no knowledge of their programming. In movie terms, the Manchurian candidate lives and does not even require a phone call." The DIA also suggests that telepathic hypnosis could be "targeted against U.S. or Allied personnel in nuclear missile silos,"[7] and in 1981, the air force seriously considered buying "psychic shields" for missile crewmen. The shields were produced by a member of the U.S. Psychotronics Association, the same outfit that sold the navy Charles Whitehouse and the multispectral image analyzer, and require a drop of blood or lock of hair to protect the bearer. Alan Gevins, the director of Langley Porter Neuropsychiatric Institute, the nation's leading center for brain research, offered the air force "transistorized cloves of garlic" at half the price.

The most bizarre threat, according to the DIA, is the apport technique, which is "a form of astral projection in which the psychic subject transports his 'energy body' to a remote site, dematerializes an object, then transports it back and materializes it."[8] There are no reports of the Soviets planning to filch U.S. equipment this way, but the DIA called the "lack of information on Soviet interest in the technique . . . a major intelligence gap."

According to the DIA report, "Apport phenomena in which physical objects have passed through solid walls have been observed and attested to by some of the world's most eminent scientists"; among them is Sir William Crookes (1832–1919), British chemist and physicist:

> I [William Crookes] have more than once seen, first an object move, and then a luminous cloud appear to form about it, and lastly, the cloud condense into shape and become a perfectly formed hand. . . . It is not always a mere form, but sometimes appears perfectly lifelike and graceful, the fingers moving and the flesh apparently as human as that of any in the room. At the wrist or arm, it becomes hazy and fades off into a luminous cloud. To the touch, the hand sometimes appears icy cold and dead, at other times warm and lifelike, grasping my own with the firm pressure of an old friend.

"It is a known fact," according to this intelligence report, "that the Soviet Union takes the appearance of luminous bodies very seriously":

> It appears that the Soviets may be considering that a hand which appears out of nowhere and can grasp, "with the firm pressure of an old friend," another person may have first-rate military possibilities. There has been some discussion recently about being able to control the apport technique to a point of sophistication where individuals could control these "luminous clouds" . . . they might well be used to produce instant death in military and civilian officials. It is further conjectured that these bodies could disable military equipment or communication nets.

One thing is certain, the DIA report concludes: "The powers of the subconscious mind are vastly superior to those of the conscious."

Even the apport technique may be old-fashioned. "One of the things the Pentagon is studying now," according to James Randi, "is sympathetic magic. They are trying to develop high-resolution photographs of Russian installations with the idea that if they burn those photos, the satellites and missiles will be destroyed. I know that's pretty hard to take, but that's the juju boys in the Pentagon." Lieutenant Colonel Bearden claims the Soviets already have such a weapon, the "photonic barrier modulator," and used it to destroy the U.S. nuclear submarine *Thresher*, which sank mysteriously in 1963 with all hands aboard.

"Some of the [government's] interest in psi ties into the security of nuclear weapons," according to Ron Robertson, the security officer at Lawrence Livermore Laboratory in California, which designs nuclear warheads. If Uri Geller can bend spoons and keys through psychokinesis, and demonstrations Geller gave at Livermore convinced Robertson he can, then he can trigger a nuclear bomb: "All it takes is the ability to move one eighth of an ounce a quarter of an inch." Robertson estimates that the Pentagon funds between thirty and forty psychic research projects.

Outside the government, "considerable concern has been expressed lately" by serious researchers about possible military applications of parapsychology, according to a survey[9] by Charles T. Tart. Thirteen of the fourteen best-known parapsychology laboratories in the United States responded to Tart's questionnaire. Of those, none considered the use of psychic powers for espionage impossible or unlikely, assuming that very large amounts of money and scientific manpower were used to develop such applications. Four considered "ESPionage" possible, five likely, and the remaining four certain. Similar proportions of the researchers believed psychic powers might be used to physically harm, sicken, or kill individuals, or to interfere with the operation of physical equipment such as computers. In his February 1982 paper for the *Proceedings of the Institute of Electrical and Electronic Engineers,* Robert Jahn called remote viewing of clear "interest for intelligence agencies, law enforcement units, and any other activity relying on surveillance."[10]

Five of the laboratories in Tart's survey had been officially approached by the U.S. government for parapsychology information.

The potential military use of psi does not depend on achieving such spectacular effects as the apport technique, telepathic hypnosis, or even bending keys. It would be reassuring if it did, for it is easy to believe that those effects will never be seen outside the movie theater. Many researchers, discouraged by the continual exposures of "psychics" such as Uri Geller and M.E. and S.S. as frauds, have abandoned tests of spectacular effects and concentrated on tests of low-energy psychokinesis, called micro-PK. Typically, the psychic subject tries to influence a simple mechanical or electrical system, such as a sensitive thermometer or computer microchip, which can be affected by a very low level of energy. Researchers such as Robert Jahn say such tests have shown consistently positive results.

At first glance, it should make little difference to the military that psychics might be able to affect circuits controlled by a few thousandths of a volt, when the next war might be fought with nuclear weapons that explode with the force of 20 million tons of TNT. But H-bombs explode only after dozens of computers have ordered them to do so—computers that code the orders to fire and transmit them to missile crews, decode the firing orders in the silo fail-safe box, guide the missile through space, and arm the warhead. Each of those computers is controlled by tiny electronic circuits, each of which can be disrupted by a few thousandths of a volt. In fact, virtually every modern weapon—radar, smart bombs, aircraft navigation systems, even the gunsight on a tank—depends utterly on computers. Psychic control of computers would indeed be analogous to a nuclear monopoly, and this fact has not escaped the attention of the Pentagon.

The apparent ability of talented psychics to jam computers and the military implications have inspired a degree of paranoia in the parapsychology community. One of the psychics tested at Stanford Research Institute, Ingo Swann, claimed that publicizing the research might result in his assassination. Researcher Jeffrey Mishlove believes that anyone with the ability to jam computers "would probably have to be destroyed," but adds, "if this hypothetical psychic were truly talented, death probably wouldn't even stop him."

Robert Van de Castle, one of the nation's leading parapsychologists, recalls a visit from two CIA researchers. "One of the things they wanted to know," he says, "is whether Geller could jam computers."

Robert Jahn's research at Princeton University focuses on whether "the basic processes of microelectronic elements could be even slightly disturbed by intentional or inadvertent intervention of human consciousness . . . especially in situations involving high psychological stress."[11] During the Vietnam War, the navy suspected that "psychic mishandling" may have triggered a rash of mysterious bomb explosions on carriers operating in the Gulf of Tonkin. Could excited launch control officers in a missile silo inadvertently disturb the navigational computers and destroy Washington instead of Moscow? Do silos need psychic shields, or as skeptics claim, just the "transistorized clove of garlic" to calm the fears of superstitious parapsychologists? The Pentagon would certainly like to know, but for ethical reasons, Jahn and his coworkers refuse to accept "black money" from the Pentagon. Their funding, they say, comes wholly from "private sources." Unless Jahn has looked into every cavity of his gift horse's mouth, however, he is unlikely to know if his greenbacks are really black (I have no knowledge that they are). The CIA routinely launders research money through private sources, so researchers might never learn the real source of their funding. Jahn himself admits that "the extent of classified research in this country is a matter of considerable speculation on which I cannot comment with authority."[12]

A 1952 CIA memo released in 1978[13] reveals the agency decided to "push [psi] research as far and as fast as we can reasonably do in the direction of practical application" to military and intelligence problems, while being "exceedingly careful about thorough cloaking of the undertaking. Funds necessary for the support of the work would . . . carry no identification and raise no question." The cloaking policy never changed, according to the funding officer[14] responsible for covert parapsychology research funding in the late seventies: "For the most part the agency just doesn't want to be embarrassed, but there are other considerations as well." Stanley Krippner did not learn that the private half (the public half was a National Institute of Health grant) of his funding for the 1975 Maimonides experiments with Shawn Robbins and others came from a CIA office until seven years later: "I read about it in a magazine article."

Concealing the source of funds from psychics poses special problems. If the psychics are genuine, the agency reasons, they might learn the truth telepathically from the middleman or sense "psychic fingerprints" on documents that had been prepared in the agency headquarters. On the other hand, if the psychics did not pick up the clues, they could not be genuine and the project was therefore a waste of money. The CIA solves this dilemma by using two middlemen for psychic funding, one who knows the CIA connection and another who believes the cover story. Such "double-blind" security precautions are unusual, even for the most dangerous overseas counterintelligence operations.

Few of the unclassified research projects in this country are of such obvious interest to the military as Jahn's work. Most researchers are attempting to prove psi exists and do so with an experiment that can be repeated and verified by skeptical researchers. Currently the most promising attempts involve random-number generators, pioneered by Helmut Schmidt at the Mind Science Foundation near San Antonio, Texas, and Charles Honorton at the Psychophysical Research Laboratory in Princeton, New Jersey.

Random-number generators resemble an arcade video game, with flashing lights and zapping sounds. The sound and light displays are controlled by the decay of a radioactive substance. There is no process more random than radioactivity. Scientists can calculate approximately *how many* atoms will emit radiation over a given period of time, but cannot predict precisely *when* radiation will be emitted. In theory, a psychic subject cannot control the display without controlling the radioactive decay, an impossible task unless micro-psychokinesis exists—mind over matter at an atomic level.

These experiments have numerous advantages over tests with subjects like Geller. First, radioactive decay cannot be influenced by prestidigitation or any other means known to modern science, so the machines should be less vulnerable to cheating. Second, if psychic abilities are part of the human makeup, the abilities of untalented as well as gifted subjects should be measurable at the atomic level. Third, the results on the machine can be quantified and tabulated, allowing sophisticated statistical analysis to determine if the scores are likely to be the result of chance or so unlikely some unknown causal factor, psi, must be at work.

Honorton calls his machine "Psi Trek"; it is designed to look and feel like a game, to make the test exciting. The display is divided into four quadrants. The subject aims his ray guns at one, trying to outguess enemy flying saucers. If he guesses correctly, the enemy saucer explodes in orange and blue and the machine signals "Direct hit!" The arcade paraphernalia does more than lure young subjects to the laboratory; Honorton and other parapsychologists theorize that psi operates better when the subject is relaxed and spontaneous. Analytical, doubting subjects score consistently lower. Parapsychologists refer to the goat and sheep effect; sheep, the believers, consistently score well; while goats, the skeptics, do not.[15]

Some researchers suggest the effect may account for the failure of skeptical researchers to duplicate successful ESP experiments.

Honorton introduced another promising advance in psi experimental methods: the "Ganzfeld," or sensory shielding technique, which, in combination with random-number generators, at least eight laboratories in the United States and Great Britain claim has produced the best and most consistent results of any experimental method to date. Ganzfeld experimenters shield the subjects from as many distracting influences as possible, even placing half Ping-Pong balls over their eyes, in order to reduce any sensory "noise" interfering with the extrasensory signal.

There are more conventional theories in physics that percolate happily on much weaker statistical grounds than those claimed by the Ganzfeld experimenters, but unregenerate skeptics remain. The random-number generators have not proved invulnerable to cheating, according to Randi who claims he controlled one machine by stomping on the electric cord. Another magician I consulted disputed Randi's claim: "It sounds silly to me and makes no sense anyway, since the random output from the radioactive substance is not electrically juiced anyway." Randi, he said, "shoots from the hip." Sometimes he hits the mark; sometimes he misses.

The strongest attack on the latest experiments comes from a statistician, Persi Diaconis of Stanford University. Diaconis is a leading statistician and also the "Black Bart" of magicians. He never performs publicly and rarely even for other magicians, but is reputed to be among the world's best card magicians.

Diaconis has criticized the statistical analysis of the random-number generator experimental data and, more generally, the statistical methods used by parapsychology researchers for the past fifteen years.

One of the most common early ESP experiments involves

guessing "Zenar cards," a deck of twenty-five cards, including five with squares, five with triangles, five with circles, five with wavy horizontal lines, and five with straight vertical lines. Common sense says that a person stands to guess five right; consistently more than the expected five correct guesses, or "hits," should indicate the presence of some information transfer, or ESP. Literally hundreds of prestigious experiments reported in parapsychology journals over the last fifteen years took the commonsense approach. Robert Morris, one of the best-known researchers, expressed the hope that better experimental designs would produce more convincing proofs than "the ordinary garden variety of laboratory induced 5.75 right out of 25 generally shown on standard ESP cards."[16]

Unfortunately, the commonsense approach doesn't work; *not a single one* of the over five hundred articles Diaconis surveyed reached valid statistical conclusions. The "garden variety" proof of ESP is not a proof at all; Diaconis showed that the number of expected guesses is much higher. Five hundred experiments claimed to show ESP; in fact, their results were uniformly at or below chance. A huge literature and thousands of hours of effort must be dicarded due to a statistical error, which, as Diaconis explains it, should be obvious to anyone who takes card games seriously.

Diaconis calculated that the number of expected correct guesses in Zenar card tests varies according to how the experiment is conducted. If the subject guesses the first card is a circle, and is told, "You're right! It was a circle," he knows there are only four circles left in the deck, but five of everything else. The odds that the second card is a circle are therefore four out of the twenty-four remaining cards, and the odds on everything else slightly better, five out of twenty-four. Every time a card is played, the subject knows more, and a competent card player should guess seven or eight cards right.

The odds change again if the subject is told only he guessed right or wrong, and not what the card was. For example, if you guess that the first card is a circle and are wrong, the best strategy is to guess circle again on the second card. You know there are five circles left in the cards; there may be only four of anything else. The mathematics to find the expected number of hits under all these circumstances cover twenty pages.

Some parapsychologists have claimed that Diaconis did not review the most current experimental data. Diaconis counters that he reviewed "all the published experiments in the parapsychology journals.

"It's very difficult to have a fruitful scientific dialogue," says Diaconis, "particularly when you try to be constructively critical. Most parapsychologists don't have the statistical expertise to interpret the experiments they're doing, and some just can't accept outside help. The same can be said of scientists in other fields."

Complex as the statistical interpretations of Zenar card experiments are, compared to the difficulty of interpreting the results of the random-number generator experiments, they are remedial arithmetic. Those results raise fundamental questions of statistical theory and according to Robert Jahn, "are vulnerable to . . . impressionistic bias and argument."[17]

Naturally, although statisticians cannot say unequivocally that the random-number trials prove the existence of psi, neither can they offer an alternative explanation. The mathematics simply defy current understanding. It is therefore fair to say, as does Robert Jahn, that the random-number and Ganzfeld experiments do suggest things "currently inexplicable in terms of established science." They suggest, Jahn cautions, but they do not prove: "I am aware of no reputable investigator who has claimed, let alone demonstrated, any psychic experiment approaching classical scientific replicability."[18]

It has become almost a cliché that the Soviets do not conduct experiments such as these, designed to prove that psi really exists.

According to the authors of the CIA's 1976 review of Soviet

psi research, in which the CIA scientists themselves avoid using the word *psi* by referring to "novel biological information transfer" (NBIT), "The Soviets do not undertake studies . . . in which remote card reading or other simple telepathic tests are carried out repeatedly to gather statistical evidence. The Soviets assume the reality of thought transference. Their best experiments are designed to elucidate the physical basis of these NBIT mechanisms."[19]

Parapsychology research in the United States concentrates on compiling statistical evidence for the existence of psi because that approach has the best chance of overcoming the objections of the U.S. scientific establishment, and not because parapsychology researchers themselves necessarily think such experiments are the most interesting. In fact, researchers polled at the 1981 Parapsychology Association convention generally thought statistical experiments *less* interesting than Soviet-style experiments designed to elucidate the mechanism of psi. Few Soviet-style experiments are done in this country because it is difficult to obtain funding to explore the mechanism of psi when its very existence is politically controversial in the scientific community.

I should not be surprised if a poll of Soviet researchers found that they preferred the American experiments. Soviet experimenters fight a different bias, a bias that favors mechanical explanations of reality to the discovery of new mysteries. This bias dictates that rather than attempt statistical tests to prove a "bourgeois superstition" exists, the Soviet researcher must assume psi exists and show that Western scientists have misinterpreted natural phenomena, a mechanism understandable in terms of the official materialist philosophy. Experiments of the Western type are not uninteresting but rather politically unacceptable in the Soviet Union.

To some degree, the differences in the experiments are semantic. American researchers sidestep occult connotations with circumlocutions such as "novel biological information transfer systems" or "noncognitive levels of awareness." Soviet researchers

talk about "paraphysics" or "bioplasma" rather than parapsychology or invisible auras. Some of the differences in experimental
procedure reflect other cultural biases. Card games are unpopular,
considered "bourgeois," in the Soviet Union (as they were in
Poland, until recently—it is perhaps a sign of ineffective Soviet
control that the Poles now field some of the best contract bridge
teams in the world), so talented Soviet psychics are often asked
to separate the yolk from the white of an egg from a distance
rather than guess Zenar cards. There are differences between
American and Soviet research, but not fundamental differences.
Scientists in both nations stalk an elusive, mysterious, and politically controversial prey.

Strongly held beliefs about parapsychology have had the effect
of discouraging research in this country too, even when the projects in question arguably had nothing to do with psi. In 1977,
Samuel Koslov, assistant secretary of the navy for research and
development, learned the navy had a contract with Stanford
Research Institute to study ELF and mind control. "ELF" stands
for extremely low frequency radio waves. Because the human
brain generates electrical signals in the same frequencies, scientists speculate that transmitting strong signals in these frequencies might interfere with the natural brain activity of persons in
the target area, producing effects ranging from hypertension to
sudden death. But the "mind control" label upset Koslov, who
rejects anything that smacks of psi and the occult. He ordered all
navy-funded psi research stopped. The SRI contract was canceled, but other projects avoided the ax. Currently, research on
the effects of ELF on the human brain are well funded and highly
classified.

Despite virulent opponents like Koslov, researchers in this
country have won the political support necessary to secure at least
nominal federal funding. A June 1981 staff report for the House
Committee on Science and Technology endorsed psi research,
arguing that

research on the physics of consciousness has received relatively low funding largely because the credibility and potential yield of such research is widely questioned, although less today than ever before. . . . Given the potentially powerful and far-reaching implications of knowledge in this field, and given that the Soviet Union is widely acknowledged to be supporting such research at a far higher and more official level, Congress may wish to undertake a serious assessment of the research effort in this country.[20]

The report notes that police have used psychics to trace "emotional imprints" at crime sites, and although "there is no certainty as to what results will emerge from basic and exploratory research . . . now under way," in the area of national defense "there are obvious implications of one's ability to identify distant sites and affect sensitive instruments or other humans."

Support in Congress for parapsychology research is hardly unanimous, however. According to Tom McNamara, formerly an aide to Tennessee Congressman Robin Beard (defeated in a 1982 Senate bid), "This kind of research makes the whole defense establishment look ridiculous." When Beard heard about Madame Zodiac and the Army War College's psychics, the congressman, a colonel in the Marine Corps and then only member of Congress in the active reserve, tried to find out "what the hell is going on and why."

"Now if [the Pentagon] has a legitimate case and they can prove it in a reasonable way, then we'll just bag the investigation," McNamara told one reporter, "but it's going to have to be good, brother. Madame Zodiac is more than I can handle."[21]

Dick Giza, a member of the House Intelligence Committee staff, countered: "Considering some of the half-assed things this government has funded in the past, like studies of ethnicity in Milwaukee, Wisconsin, this is not a bad area to throw money into."

Koslov's attitude gets support from former White House plumber G. Gordon Liddy, whose official duties once included the exploitation of unconventional intelligence methods and devices. "The Russians are spending a great deal of money on parapsychology," says Liddy, "and there's a unit devoted to it in the Pentagon. I think it's bullshit, but if they want to do that, that's all right. I just hope they don't waste too much of the taxpayers money." Liddy doesn't see the research as a threat to anyone but the taxpayers: "I think the weapons of the future involve high-energy lasers, even proton accelerators and things like that. I don't see it being ESP. I think that stuff ought to be left to Stephen King."

On one occasion, the Pentagon did check up on Soviet research and confirmed at least one project was a waste of their money. In 1975, the army awarded a $145,000 contract to four physicists at Drexel University in Philadelphia to investigate Kirlian photography, named after the Soviet husband-and-wife team who discovered the process. Kirlian photographs, taken while the subject is under a high-voltage field, purport to show an "aura" of moving, flaring colors surrounding living things. "We appeared to be seeing the very life activities . . . we see the inner state of the organism reflected in the brightness, dimness, and color of the flares," said the Kirlians.

Kirlian photographs seemed to reflect the emotional state of human subjects, the colors varying to reflect anger, joy, good or poor health. Even more amazing, they seemed to photograph the soul, perhaps the source of psychic powers. A photograph of a freshly cut leaf, for example, showed the outline of the whole leaf, including the missing part—proof positive of a psychic whole, in some sense apart from material existence, claimed the Kirlians.

The Drexel report exploded that hope. The "auras" are a form of corona discharge, similar to the northern lights, caused by the interaction of the high-voltage field and moisture in the subject. "Since our work substantiates the view that the dominant source of the energy responsible for latent image formation in the usual Kirlian photography is a corona discharge," stated the authors in their final report, "we will refer to this technique as corona discharge photography."

The physicists showed that any moist object has a Kirlian aura, including bowls of spaghetti and used prophylactics. The colors do correspond to the emotional state of human subjects, because humans perspire more or less depending on stress. Lie detectors also measure minute changes in perspiration. As for the cut leaf, the Drexel scientists discovered that the electric field actually etches the image of anything photographed in the glass specimen plate—once the full leaf has been photographed, its image will remain until polished away.

Until the Drexel study, the Pentagon seriously considered using Kirlian photography in a variety of applications. The Army Material Command studied Kirlian photography as a fatigue indicator:

> Both mental fatigue and physical fatigue were included in the study. The mental stressor used was engineering graduate school class lectures; the physical stressor was softball games played under hot, humid atmospheric conditions. The photograph parameter used to indicate fatigue was the fingertip's corona diameter.

Not surprisingly, since the Drexel study correlated the Kirlian effect with the moisture of sweat, the Army Material Command study found that the fingertip corona "increased after applying the physical stressor" (the softball game) and "decreased after applying the mental stressor" (the lecture in an air-conditioned room).

Strangely enough, the Drexel Study made little impression in the popular psychic press. The Drexel scientists were not skeptics; in fact, three of them are now attempting to verify telekenesis using lasers.

Congressman Beard never did find out what was going on. The navy informed his staff that a computer search revealed no research in the areas of "psi," "extrasensory perception," or "parapsychology." If the congressman had known to ask for "novel biological information transfer systems" or "remote sensing of (faint) electromagnetic stimuli at a noncognitive level of awareness," the computer might have been more helpful.

Does all this—the doomsday intelligence estimates, indications that psychics can sabotage computers, dematerialize warheads, and remotely view any secret document, open support in Congress for a federal commitment to psychic research—make a psychic arms race?

Obviously, skeptics say no, it makes, at most, a mutual delusion. Samuel Koslov, the assistant secretary of the navy who tried unsuccessfully to eliminate psychic research, dislikes even the mention of so-called psychic weapons. "This sort of talk encourages people to take off on wild-goose chases," he says. "If the Soviets are really wasting any money on this nonsense, they are doing it because their newspapers reported that *we* had opened a psychic arms gap. I can show you the clippings."

Press reports on parapsychology are, to say the least, overwrought, even in the Soviet Union. "Typical of both Soviet and foreign publications," complained one Soviet critic, "are the mutual exaggerations of the results obtained":

Judging from reports in the American press, in the USSR in 1966 there were organized and conducted telepathic séances for long-distance communications—Moscow to Novosibirsk and Moscow to Leningrad—with positive and reliable results obtained, which is sheer fiction.

In its turn, in *Komsomol'skaya Pravda,* there was a report about the fact that at the time of the telepathic séance Earth to *Apollo 14,* positive results were obtained. Edgar Mitchell, the organizer and a participant in these experiments, wrote that negative results were obtained and, moreover, that the number of successes was much lower than one could expect according to the theory of probability.[22]

Numerous popular publications in the United States duplicated *Komsomol'skaya Pravda*'s erroneous accounts of the ESP tests astronaut Edgar Mitchell conducted during his flight to the moon, but sensational and sloppy reporting on psychic events spans the spectrum, from the grocery store yellow sheets to the stuffiest and most prestigious journals. On December 13, 1977, for example, the *National Enquirer,* probably hoping to ride the popularity of the hit movie *Close Encounters of the Third Kind,* which was released that month, claimed that UFOs were "spotted at nuclear bases and missile sites." A year later, *Parade* magazine published the same story under the headline UFOS VS. USAF: AMAZING (BUT TRUE) ENCOUNTERS. A month after *Parade,* the *Washington Post* featured the story on the front page as "What Were Those Mysterious Craft?" The story made the newspaper of record nine months later, when *The New York Times Magazine* declared in "UFO Files: The Untold Story," that, "Though officials have long denied that they take 'flying saucers' seriously, declassified documents now reveal extensive Government concern over the phenomenon."

I often wonder why reporters who make a crusade of labeling government agencies inefficient, corrupt, and misguided treat classified documents from those same agencies as if they were the dead sea scrolls. One can not believe everything one reads, whether it is labeled "all the news that's fit to print" or "top secret." In this case, the reporters apparently misread the documents. Their real "untold story" was that individuals interested in UFOs never convinced the government with a capital "G," although they did try hard for twenty years.

According to one Defense Intelligence Agency report,[23] neither our own popular press nor the intelligence agencies themselves are "shy about assigning specific numbers to the level" of Soviet funding of psi research. "In one form or another, the estimate of 12 to 20 million rubles (or dollars) has survived for at least the last decade and recurs as a current estimate routinely, despite the fact that no one knows, or is saying, how it was originally derived." That estimate, the report concludes, is "if anything, grossly inflated."

Nevertheless, the bottom line is that parapsychology is in fact undergoing a revival, both in the United States and the Soviet Union. The official Soviet encyclopedia no longer defines *parapsychology* as an "antiscientific, idealistic fiction," as it did under Stalin; the most recent edition defines *parapsychology* as "a field of investigations studying primarily (1) forms of sensitivity that serve as a means for the reception of information and that cannot be explained by the activity of known sense organs, and (2) corresponding forms of action of a living organism on physical phenomena originating outside the organism without the use of muscular effort." As long as they conform to the mechanistic language of "paraphysics" and "biofields," Soviet researchers are free to discuss even miraculous cures and psychic plants:

> The further deciphering of psychophysical and biophysical enigmas will make it possible to explain certain phenomena in the history of religion that are still unexplained. We already know that healing is performed not by "holy" water but by water that has been irradiated by biofields. Certain plots of land on which churches have been built may have the same effect.
>
> The American researcher C. Backster, who has made various experiments with plants, claims that they are capable of perceiving human emotions—grief, joy, etc. Actually, however, plants are sensitive not to emotions as such but to biofields. If a person is embittered, his field is "aggressive"; it affects the biofields of plants and is registered by them. Green plants that have "witnessed" criminal acts convey very important information, which an experienced person with extrasensory powers can decipher.[24]

The opinions of the many eminent scientists in both nations who believe parapsychology research may lead to fundamental new discoveries cannot be entirely ignored. The Pentagon has a legitimate interest and indeed a statutory responsibility to investigate the military implications of this research. On at least two occasions, as we shall see, military interest in the psychic arms race reached the pinnacle of the defense establishment—the White House and the National Security Agency.

NOTES

1. Sheila Ostrander and Lynn Schroeder, *Psychic Discoveries Behind the Iron Curtain,* 1970.
2. *Proceedings and Debates of the 92nd Congress,* First Session, Vol. 117, November 17, 1971.
3. *Soviet and Czechoslovakian Parapsychology Research,* DIA, Washington, D.C., 1975.
4. *Controlled Offensive Behavior,* DIA, Washington, D.C., 1972.
5. Edward C. Wortz, J. W. Eerkens et al., "Novel Biological Information Transfer Systems," AiResearch Manufacturing Co., Torrence, California, 1976.
6. Thomas Bearden, "Soviet Psychotronic Weapons," *Specula,* October 1978.
7. *Soviet and Czechoslovakian Parapsychology Research,* op. cit., p. 30.
8. Ibid., p. 55.
9. Charles T. Tart, "A Survey of Potentially Negative Uses of Psi," University of California at Davis, 1979.
10. Robert Jahn, "The Persistent Paradox of Psychic Phenomena: An Engineering Perspective," *Proceedings of the IEEE,* February 1982, p. 164.
11. Ibid.
12. Ibid., p. 139.
13. A number of documents related to CIA-sponsored research in parapsychology were released to the Church of Scientology during legal arguments over the church's alleged spying on the federal government and counterallegations that the government had, among other things, used psychics to spy on the church.
14. The officer recently retired from the CIA and agreed to an interview with two conditions: (1) he is not identified by name, and (2) the CIA reviewed portions of this book derived from that interview and had the option to delete classified material.

15. Honorton, in the *Zetetic Scholar,* Number 8, p. 34.
16. Diaconis, "Statistical Problems in ESP Research," in *Science,* October 1981.
17. Jahn, op. cit., p. 140.
18. Ibid., p. 141.
19. Henry C. Wortz et al., "An Investigation of Soviet Psychical Research," in *Mind at Large,* edited by Charles C. Tart, Harold Puthoff, and Russell Targ, 1981.
20. *Survey of Science and Technology Issues, Present and Future,* June 1981, p. 59.
21. "Pentagon Putting Its Mind to Psychic Arms Race," *Minneapolis Star,* October 6, 1981, p. B1.
22. W. P. Zinchenko et. al., "Parapsychology: Fact or Fiction?", in *The Signet Handbook of Parapsychology,* edited by Martin Ebon, p. 459.
23. December 10, 1978.
24. *Trud,* April 23, 1980.

4 · THE MAGICIAN AND THE SCIENTISTS

It was the legend of Uri Geller that first brought parapsychology and the best minds in the science establishment together for the first time. Renowned physicists pronounced Geller genuine. Edgar Mitchell, one of the first astronauts to walk on the moon, promoted him. Even an American president received him, and listened to his message—the United States must match Soviet strides in psychic warfare or forfeit the world.

President Jimmy Carter met Geller at the 1976 inauguration of Mexican president José Lopez Portillo. Geller bent Mrs. Rosalynn Carter's fork, earning an invitation to meet privately with the Carters at the conclusion of the dinner.

Jimmy Carter liked Geller, and Geller performs best for approving audiences—disapproval, in fact, often provokes pouts, tears, and the notorious Geller temper tantrum. Geller offered to read the president-elect's mind.

Carter was told to write the name of any object that came into his mind on a pad of paper; Geller could see only the outside of the pad. By watching the movements of the arm, magicians can tell exactly what the subject writes—a feat so common it is known in the trade as "the pencil-reading," but still effective. Carter was convinced that Geller was a genuine psychic and listened seriously to Geller's warnings about the Soviet lead in the psychic arms race. Carter left the inauguration more determined than ever to focus some attention on UFOs and the psychic threat at the Pentagon.

Quite apart from Geller's claims, President Carter had good reasons in 1976 to believe that the Soviets, at least, took psychic warfare seriously. Just before the Carter inauguration, the KGB abruptly turned off mysterious microwave radiation that the KGB had beamed at the U.S. embassy in Moscow since the mid-sixties. The radiations fell well under the U.S. standard for a health risk, but exceeded the much lower Soviet standard.

The State Department insisted that it had "no proof" the radiation was harmful, but allowed complaining employees to transfer for health reasons. A private study commissioned by the department found evidence of a link between the bombardment and an abnormal incidence of cancer among embassy employees "inconclusive."

The U.S. ambassador to Moscow thought the microwaves were being used to monitor conversations within the embassy, and *The New York Times* reported that the Soviets hoped to interfere with American spy devices that had eavesdropped on conversations between the Kremlin and officials who had radio telephones in their limousines. Neither explanation impresses intelligence experts I consulted; technically, according to the best understanding in this country, the microwaves could neither monitor conversations nor interfere with electronic equipment within the embassy.

A spokesman for the State Department told me "serious consideration" was given to two other hypotheses. First, the Soviets might have deliberately attempted to affect the health of embassy employees. The second possibility is even more bizarre: The Americans might have been the targets of electronic mind control.

The record of Soviet psi research before World War II lends credence to these hypotheses. Before Stalin clamped the lid on "antimaterialist" psychic research, Professor Leonid L. Vasiliev, the head of the Department of Physiology at the University of Leningrad, published *Experiments in Distant Influence,* a pioneering attempt to show that ESP exists and operates through the entirely natural, and therefore acceptable to doctrinaire material-

ists, medium of electromagnetic waves. Quite apart from its interest to parapsychologists, the work of Vasiliev and his colleagues
was among the first to show that even very low-level radiation can
affect living organisms and cause dizziness, loss of appetite, emotional instability, and hallucinations. Vasiliev also hypothesized
that thoughts can be grafted onto microwaves in the same way
television signals carry pictures and sound, opening the possibility
of long-distance hypnosis or mind control.

Carter was undoubtedly briefed on the Moscow microwaves,
but the status of parapsychology research in the Soviet Union at
the time was as mysterious as the radiations. In 1975, apparently
outraged by "anti-Sovietism" in the book *Psychic Discoveries
Behind the Iron Curtain* and Voice of America broadcasts of
excerpts, the Soviets had charged the authors' most important
Soviet contact, Eduard Naumov, with accepting fees for lectures
without permission and sentenced him to two years in a labor
camp. During the trial, the prosecution emphasized Naumov's
connections with Western parapsychologists. Afterward, his colleagues were dismissed from their jobs. Publicly visible psychic
research in the Soviet Union shut down for the first time since
the Stalin restrictions were loosened in 1961.

But did psychic research disappear or just become invisible?
About the time Carter became president, a growing number of
Soviet emigrants were claiming the Soviets had secret parapsychology laboratories for police and military purposes. August
Stern, an emigrant physicist, said in 1977 that he spent three
years in the late 1960s trying to find the physical basis for psychic
energy, or "psi particles," as Soviet theorists called them. The
laboratory at Science City in Novosibirsk had a separate building,
a coded lock, and was known as "Special Department No. 8," a
branch of the Institute of Automation and Electrometry. Sixty
scientists were given "unlimited funds," according to Stern, and
experimented by giving electric shocks to newborn kittens to see
if their mothers showed any reaction three floors away, using
television surveillance of people to see if they responded to distant

hypnosis, and putting bacteria between two sheets of glass to see if disease could be transmitted through the glass. The Science City laboratory closed in 1969, but Stern learned that the research had been transferred to a KGB laboratory in Moscow.

Nikolai Khokhlov was a KGB agent sent to West Germany in the fifties armed with a gun disguised as a pack of cigarettes and ordered to kill an exiled dissident. Instead, he defected. In 1976, the CIA asked Khokhlov to prepare a report on secret Soviet parapsychology research centers. Khokhlov claims there are at least twenty, manned by "the best scientists with the best equipment."

Lev Tummerman, a physicist who emigrated to Israel, claimed the Soviets had offered him 10 million rubles to finance the study of psychic mind control in 1969, a few years before he emigrated: "Everything you need, people, money, equipment, buildings, everything."

In 1977 Soviet parapsychology research finally became an issue the Carter administration could not ignore, no matter how skeptical some officials remained. On June 11, the KGB arrested *Los Angeles Times* reporter Robert C. Toth in Moscow and charged him with obtaining a "secret" state document, which revealed the existence of ongoing research in parapsychology at several laboratories in the Soviet Union. The Soviet newspaper *Tass* accused Toth of acting for "American special agencies."

On that night, Toth's contact, Valery G. Petukhov of the Institute for Biomedical Problems, called him at his hotel and asked to meet him immediately on a corner across the street from the hotel. Just as Petukhov handed Toth a twenty-page paper on psi particles, the KGB pulled up in a Soviet-built Fiat and arrested them both. According to *Tass*, Toth hoped to use Petukhov as "a regular and clandestine source of secret materials from a laboratory of an institute of a secret character."

Petukhov remained in custody four days, and Toth was interrogated a total of twelve hours over several days of house arrest at his hotel. Toth returned home after strong U.S. protests. Carter national security adviser Zbigniew Brzezinski expressed concern that Toth's arrest raised "certain fundamental principles—the free flow of information, free access, and freedom of the press." The Soviet press saw the issue differently:

> The question would seem to be clear: There is full proof of the correspondent's illicit activity. However, the American press is depicting Toth as an "innocent victim of illegal persecution" and a victim of "intimidation." He himself has hinted significantly that he fears for his future in Moscow. "California's hero," the "fearless" and "irreproachable knight," he was feted upon his return as though he were Orpheus escaped from the underworld. Glorifying Toth's behavior in every possible way and depicting it as an achievement [was] Jack Anderson, well-known (chiefly for his close links with the American intelligence service; he does not even conceal them and likes to stress them). . . . Certain highly placed U.S. officials . . . declared that the supposedly bad treatment of him raises the issue of certain fundamental principles of the free flow of information, free access (to its sources), and freedom of the press.

Soviet outrage over slurs against their justice system and socialist concept of freedom of the press shouldn't surprise anyone. What is surprising is that the stories admitted for the first time *current* official Soviet interest in the military potential of parapsychology:

> It transpires that Mr. Toth's friend is not merely an amateur of parapsychology. He runs the laboratory of an institute. And it was no accident that the meetings with him were fixed conspiratorially in secluded corners—Toth, to use the bare language of the documents of the investigation, was striving to transform his acquaintance into a source for obtaining espionage information. And here he was extremely interested in the activity of one institution—the kind of institution whose affairs ought to be known only to a narrow circle of people. . . .
> His [Toth's] "sources" were people who were perfectly aware of

Mr. Toth's predilection for the sectors of science having a military application.

Never has the U.S. government made such an admission, although, as we have seen, the United States does conduct such research. Whenever our government has released military research on parapsychology, under the Freedom of Information Act or whatever, it has been ten-year-old research, long discredited and of no real interest to anyone, let alone a spy. Freedom of the press was obviously not the only issue involved in the Toth affair.

At the National Security Council meetings during Toth's detention, President Carter raised other issues. He had disappointed UFO enthusiasts by failing to deliver as he promised during the campaign undisclosed government files on UFOs. Uri Geller had warned him that the Soviets screened children for psychic abilities and might amass an army of psychic supermen. Now Toth had been arrested for receiving state secrets in a science that some of Carter's advisers claimed didn't exist. Carter ordered a new, definitive intelligence estimate of Soviet psychic research and its military potential, using all the intelligence resources available to the CIA, the first such report ever done at the pinnacle of the U.S. national security establishment.

In retrospect, it seems Toth was set up, lured into a clumsy street encounter, and nabbed by lurking KGB agents. Stansfield Turner, the director of the CIA at the time, has always believed that "the evidence points to a frame-up." But why entrap Toth for psychic spying? No one seems to know; Turner won't even guess. The arrest of a prominent American reporter on phony spy charges surely required high-level Kremlin approval; it could not be a maneuver by lower level factions in the bureaucracy to support (or condemn) psi research. The effect of the arrest was to confirm that the Soviets did indeed support psychic research, but perhaps the KGB planned a triple double cross: frame Toth, and make the Americans think the Soviets supported psychic research when they really had no interest in the field.

The understandable concern of President Carter, whose mind Uri Geller apparently was able to read, along with some other open-minded members of the National Security Council staff, that the Soviets were using psychic spies might be justified even if all psychics are charlatans. A certain percentage of the Soviet emigrants are KGB plants, moles the Soviets hope will eventually reach important positions in their new homelands. Not all of the moles go to the United States; Israel is also a preferred target, because it has access to the newest American technology, and because so many Soviet Jews emigrate there and rise to high posts.

Emigrants with military research experience are routinely debriefed in both nations, so some intelligence officials, including both skeptics and believers in parapsychology, speculate that the KGB hopes to use parapsychology as an entrée to the American and Israeli intelligence and military research communities. The arrest of Toth increased the value of the emigrant's alleged scientific experience in the Soviet Union, they suspect, and might be seen by the KGB as a means of gaining faster access to Western laboratories and military secrets, particularly in Israel. Because mysticism is an important part of the Jewish religious tradition, an interest in parapsychology is more common among the Israeli than the U.S. scientific elite and does not carry the kinky connotations that might bar an immigrant from promising posts in the United States.

The conclusions of the comprehensive intelligence report Carter ordered were as ambiguous as the Toth case. The CIA report, completed in 1978 and partially released under the Freedom of Information Act two years later, found no evidence of a massive Soviet "psycho-warfare" project such as Geller alleged. The report emphasized, in fact, that Soviet parapsychologists face serious ideological opposition:

The Communist claim to be a scientific understanding of history is based upon the materialist doctrine. Should that fail, or be shown to have major exception, then the foundations of the Communist party and one-party government would be open to serious challenge. The point was not missed by party ideologues. By at least one line of reasoning, the phenomena which compose paraphysics can be understood to imply the existence of nonmaterial causality; it is but a short step to the anathema: the supernatural.

Soviet parapsychologists counter by asserting that the phenomena occur through material mechanisms. "Lengthy sections devoted to ideology and quotations from Lenin," the CIA noted, "are frequently found in the work of [Soviet] paraphysicists."

The CIA did find clear evidence of Soviet interest in technologies U.S. scientists would not hesitate to label psychic. Soviet dowsers prospect for oil and minerals. Soviet psychologists have tested "remote physiological monitors," devices that apparently measure the heartbeat and breathing rate of persons thousands of miles away without any known means of communication.

Nor did the CIA dismiss entirely the most apocalyptic allegations of secret Soviet psi research. Such reports, the analysts concluded, *may* be true, but the evidence is fragmentary and contradictory at best.

The same might be said of psi research in the United States.

Uri Geller's relative influence on Jimmy Carter can only be guessed at. The president's immediate concern in the National Security Council meetings was the arrest of Toth itself; intelligence reports pointing to the existence of secret Soviet psychic research could wait. But Geller's influence with the world scientific community is both crystal clear and enormous: He was almost solely responsible for an explosion of interest in psi in the early 1970s.

British Nobel laureate Brian Josephson endorsed Geller, along with other world-class physicists like Eugene Wigner and David

Bohm. John G. Taylor, one of the world's leading mathematicians, declared, "The Geller effect of metal-bending is clearly not brought about by fraud." (Taylor later recanted and denounced parapsychology as superstition.) Astronaut Edgar Mitchell swears Geller materialized a tie clasp in his ice cream. The clasp was unique, given to Mitchell by an archery company and lost three years before he met Geller. "I know it happened," says Mitchell. "A hoax is impossible."

Geller was "discovered" in Israel in 1971 by Andrija Puharich, an expert in medical electronics. Puharich understands magic; he invented the tooth radio, with which magicians send and receive messages from stage assistants. His interest in psychic warfare began during World War II. In 1952, he presented a paper on "An Evaluation of the Possible Uses of Extrasensory Perception in Psychological Warfare" to a secret Pentagon gathering. A year later he lectured air force researchers on methods of increasing or decreasing telepathy and the staff of the Army Chemical Center on the "Biological Foundations of Extrasensory Perception." Since then, he has tested one psychic after another trying to find a messiah who would convince the skeptical scientific community. It was Puharich who brought the Dutchman Peter Hurkos to the United States. Hurkos's police work won him some renown, but not the acclaim of the scientists, which Puharich sought.

"Uri is the answer to my prayers," Puharich said. "He's the something I've looked for, for thirty years."

Geller says he was "born with these powers" on December 20, 1946, the same day, according to Jewish accounts, that Jesus was born. Jesus, Geller says, also "had powers."

His psychic career began after his discharge from the Israeli army in 1968. He worked at a textile factory, sorting English, Hungarian, and Greek purchase orders, and moonlighted modeling underwear and performing "psychic" feats he had practiced as a teenager. Soon his act earned a hundred Israeli pounds a night (about thirty-eight dollars, but more than a week's salary at the factory). Geller quit, hired a manager, and launched his lucrative show-biz career. His fame soon attracted the attention of Puharich.

Geller told Puharich his powers were a gift of "the nine," the rulers of an intergalactic civilization that had selected Geller as their ambassador to earth. One of the nine (could they be the same nine the original 007, John Dee, contacted through his shew stone?) spoke to Puharich and Geller from the planet Hoova through cassette tape recorders that started spontaneously and played a "cold mechanical voice":

> We shall tell you why war-mindedness is generated, why it is fostered. Obviously, war-mindedness could be counteracted without propaganda and the threat method and mutual competitive method. For instance, we might tell you how atomic explosions, even when they are produced, can be silenced. We don't have a counteratomic weapon to fight with, but no atomic weapon will ever have any effect.[1]

Puharich thinks earthlings are mere Hoovian pets. Most of the researchers who worked with Geller said the flying saucer story didn't bother them, except when Geller dragged them around desolate country roads in the middle of the night to witness a landing.

Recently, Geller has disavowed the Hoovians. In a 1982 interview, he admitted that UFOs "detract from my credibility."

Geller gave demonstrations at NASA's Goddard Space Center and at the Lawrence Livermore nuclear weapons facility. Eldon Byrd, who describes his work as "predicting what war will be like in the future," tested Geller extensively at the top secret Naval Surface Weapons laboratory. The principals all insist the visits were unofficial, although representatives of the intelligence communities attended "discreetly."

Harold Puthoff and Russell Targ at the Stanford Research Institute (SRI) did the most extensive tests. Pressured by congressmen worried about the putative psycho-gap with the Soviet Union, the Pentagon's Advanced Research and Projects Agency

(ARPA, now renamed DARPA) decided to evaluate Geller at SRI in 1972 to determine if further testing warranted Pentagon money.

The ARPA evaluation team consisted of George Lawrence, deputy director of human resources at ARPA, psychologist Ray Hyman, and Robert Van de Castle, past president of the Parapsychology Association. Lawrence was "fully prepared to fund" the Geller experiments; personally, he considered psychokinesis "ridiculous" but was open to the possibility of "some sort of information transfer." His boss, Air Force Col. Austin Kibler, had seen Geller earlier and had been impressed. Hyman was a skeptic and, unknown to Geller, an experienced magician.

The inspection bombed from its inception. For the first time in recorded history, the temperature in Eugene, Oregon, dropped below zero, snow closed the airport, and Hyman was forced to take a 3:00 A.M. bus to Portland to catch a plane to get a car to drive to SRI. He arrived late.

Lawrence and Van de Castle spent the previous night in the area, eating a Chinese dinner. The next morning Lawrence, groaning, "It must have been the black mushrooms and seaweed," suffered Mao's revenge. Since SRI's funding depended on impressing Lawrence, runners kept him informed in the men's room about Geller's successes.

The runners couldn't have been as busy as Lawrence; Geller had few successes. He tried the pad trick, covering his eyes with his hands while the evaluators wrote numbers on a pad. Hyman saw him peek. He deflected a compass five degrees; Lawrence deflected it forty-five degrees by imitating Geller's motions, including stomping on the floor. He bent a nail clipper; Hyman bent it back.

Hyman finally suggested that Geller, Puthoff, and Targ be sent on a tour of the Soviet Union, in the hope that they defect. Van de Castle wanted to test Geller at his own laboratory, where controls could be more strict. Lawrence's opinion of Geller was negative, even truculent, but, conscious of the congressional pressure to do something about psychic research, he decided to try again.

The next day, Lawrence returned to SRI with Gerry Shure, a UCLA psychologist. Shure, like Hyman, is a practicing magician, but this time Geller was told.

Shure confronted Geller with the magician's techniques to duplicate his performance. Geller exploded: "People who do not believe and don't give a chance to people who have powers to express themselves, who immediately talk about magic, cheap card tricks . . . this is the reason that Russia is going to beat the shit out of America in psychic research!"[2]

Shure thinks Geller "duped" Puthoff and Targ. Lawrence now considers him a fraud.

According to Puthoff, "SRI's view of the ARPA debacle was that the ARPA team's 'experiments' with Geller were sloppy, uncontrolled, and did give Geller every opportunity to cheat. We, Puthoff and Targ, were incensed that these 'experiments' should in any way be laid at SRI's door, and have said so in print."

Five years after the first disastrous evaluation, Geller returned to ARPA, which was again "fully prepared to fund research," according to officials there.

Geller met with naval intelligence officials around the pool of a Virginia motel near the Pentagon. Geller challenged one commander to think of any nearby object; the commander, no dupe, thought of a bowl of grapes behind him, so that Geller couldn't see him staring at anything. Geller scribbled something on a pad of paper and asked the name of the object. Then he handed the officer the pad, on which was written "bowl of grapes." The stunned intelligence officials recommended proposing a contract with SRI for several million dollars.

Horrified skeptics at the agency, including Lawrence, flew in a team of four magicians to debunk Geller: Randi, statistician and card expert Persi Diaconis, psychologist Ray Hyman, and sociologist Marcello Truzzi. Their reception, Diaconis recalls, was hostile, "They wanted to know why we were trying to scuttle important research."

The commander challenged the debunkers to explain Geller's apparent mind reading. The magicians were reluctant for two reasons. First, the technique is a magician's secret. Second, says Truzzi, people usually don't believe the explanations, "insisting it couldn't be done with wires even when you know it was done with wires."

This intelligence officer proved to be the exception. Reflecting, he remembered Geller had asked him the name of the object before he passed the pad, not after, as he originally recalled. The difference is crucial. Geller wrote nothing when he appeared to scribble on the pad; after the commander said "a bowl of grapes," Geller quickly penned in "bowl of grapes" with a thumbwriter, a small pen concealed under the thumbnail and well known to magicians and mentalists.

By the end of the day, the attitude of the DARPA officials had turned 180 degrees. No contract was signed, and, says Diaconis, "They were all asking whose dumb idea it was in the first place."

Geller's public reputation tarnished when "the Amazing" Randi made debunking Uri a personal crusade, a crusade that, of course, did nothing to harm Randi's own career as a magician and escape artist. Not only did Randi duplicate his tricks and use stop action to expose his use of magic during television demonstrations of his alleged "powers," he also persuaded Geller's magic coach to confess. Geller deflected a compass; Randi used the same compass to find a magnet hidden in the Israeli's ample hair. Geller bent a solid metal key; Randi's stop-action photos and close-ups clearly show a hidden vise built into Geller's massive bronze belt buckle.

Despite what diehard supporters like Dr. A. R. Owen of the University of Toronto called "some minor controversy . . . which seems to have been inspired entirely by the professional jealousy of some stage magicians," the majority of the parapsychology community has admitted Geller cheats. Most maintain that although Geller is a proven cheat, he might not cheat all the time. If psychic powers exist, there is no reason to believe that Uri Geller has been excluded. Scientifically, though, any experiment with him is suspect.

Enthusiasm for the Geller effect withered in the scientific community as a result of these exposures. Robert Jahn's 1982 survey of psi in *The Proceedings of the Institute of Electrical and Electronic Engineers* mentions him only once, in number 135 of 252 footnotes. Nevertheless, the spark he ignited in the scientific community burns hotter today than ever before.

Even Puthoff and Targ complain that their work with Geller has been overpublicized to the detriment of their more conclusive studies on remote viewing. A "principal reason" for writing *Mind Reach,* they say, was to put the Geller tests in perspective: "Although our work with Mr. Geller accounts for only 3 percent of our overall effort, it has received 97 percent of our publicity."[3] They have even suggested that Geller acted as a spy, either for the CIA or Israeli intelligence, whose mission was to test their scientific protocols for the possibility of cheating.

If anyone was surprised that eminent scientists could be fooled by a magician, it was not fellow magician James Randi. "The men of science," says Randi, "are not used to working with things that deceive them. They assume they are capable of detecting deception, but they're not. They're the first to buy the Brooklyn Bridge.

"When scientists go to the theater and see a magician pull a rabbit out of his hat, they merely shrug and say, 'That's a trick.' However, when someone like Geller from the far-off land of Israel bends a spoon for them, they call it an act of the supernatural. Quite frankly, the spoon-bending trick is infinitely easier than pulling a rabbit out of a hat. Any idiot could do it."

With dismaying regularity, scientists refuse to admit they can be tricked. Edward F. Kelly, an electrical engineer and psi researcher at Duke University, did a series of experiments in 1972 with Bill Delmore, a Yale law student renowned locally for his ability to guess playing cards. Ten years later, a survey of parapsychologists rated Delmore's performance among if not "the most evidential in the entire parapsychological literature,"[4] even though Delmore had been observed using sleight of hand by Persi Diaconis, the world's undisputed top card magician.

Diaconis observed Delmore at a Harvard University demonstration Kelly arranged, in his own words, "to secure funding for later formal experiments." Kelly nevertheless stubbornly refuses to concede that Delmore's prestidigitation—more bluntly, his attempt to defraud Harvard's Hodgson research fund—might have contaminated later experiments:

> While agreeing fully that a magician's skills are highly relevant to self-staged and nonexperimental performances, I dispute Diaconis's suggestion that the presence of a magician constitutes a necessary and sufficient condition for the integrity of experimental data. It is *unnecessary* because it is perfectly possible—indeed not at all that difficult—to design experimental conditions that are impervious to cheating by any subject including a magician. And it is *insufficient* because if positive results were forthcoming, what would prevent a sufficiently resolute skeptic from claiming that the conditions were after all inadequate, and that the subject-magician was simply more skilled than the observer-magician?

None of the parapsychologists surveyed saw fit to comment on Diaconis's widely published allegations. John Beloff, a senior lecturer at the University of Edinburgh who selected the "most evidential" experiments for the survey, asserts, "One can say without fear of contradiction that there was just no conceivable way in which the subject *could* have cheated no matter how skillful he may be at card tricks."

In fact, there is just no conceivable way a nonmagician can know what can or cannot be done through sleight of hand. Even simple effects, climbing ropes and such, which have been known to magicians for centuries, seem impossible to the uninitiated even if he has had the opportunity to handle the props. "When you need an expert on medicine," Randi likes to say, "you call a doctor, not an engineer. When you need an expert on charlatans, call a magician, not a physicist."

The March 1983 revelation of Randi's three-year-long "Psiscam" hoax, in which two magicians fooled parapsychology researchers at McDonnell laboratories, has put parapsychologists on guard. Physicist Peter Phillips, the chief victim of the scheme, agreed that the hoax was worthwhile, but Randi doubts parapsychologists can reform. His many exposures of psychic fraud haven't lessened the faith of parapsychology researchers. According to him, "When the facts conflict with their theories, they throw out the facts." The Parapsychology Association has since, however, formally recommended that researchers seek the advice of magicians.

Parapsychologists would do well to keep their guard up. Randi code-named his hoax "Project Alpha." Project Beta is already under way, he confides, and "I can go right down the alphabet."

The Soviets have criticized their own scientists on similar grounds. After the publication of *Psychic Discoveries Behind the Iron Curtain,* which alleged the Soviet government supported large-scale covert psi research, official Soviet journals counterattacked.

"The history of parapsychology is a history of exposures in which at times world-renowned scientists have participated," screamed one Soviet commentator. "Just as in religion, in parapsychology faith is more powerful than facts."

Paraspsychology really shouldn't be singled out for such criticism, either in the Soviet Union or here. Fraud, credulity, and naïveté are not unknown to mainstream sciences like physics, chemistry, and astronomy. Even Galileo fudged his data to cover variations in the planetary motion observed and predicted by his theory.

Deliberate fraud by scientists, however, is probably relatively rare. The president of the National Academy of Sciences, Philip Handler, defended the research community before a congressional committee on scientific fraud in 1981. The press has exaggerated the problem, Handler insisted, and scientific fraud occurs, when it does, "in a system that operates in an effective, democratic, and self-correcting mode."

It would be more difficult to exaggerate the power of self-delusion. Even hardened skeptics fall prey.

Ray Hyman, the psychologist who suggested that Geller be sent from SRI to the Soviet Union, once believed he could read palms. At first, his readings were strictly entertainment, part of his amateur magic act, but clients insisted he showed uncanny insight. Eventually Hyman came to believe the customers must be right. Surely the hundreds who unfailingly attested to his psychic powers couldn't all be mistaken, could they?

Well, yes, they could. Hyman found his powers were those of the charismatic showman, not the psychic, when he tried telling clients exactly the *opposite* of what he saw in their palms. The clients remained as enthusiastic as always—no matter what he said, they insisted that Hyman demonstrated uncanny insight.

Hyman himself thinks that the scientific merit of what some call "deviant" hypotheses, including parapsychology, do not get a fair hearing because the scientific community doesn't know how to respond to such proposals. In a paper for the 1980 annual meeting of the American Association for the Advancement of Science, Hyman asked the scientific community to consider how it would respond to one such bizarre proposal:

A competent and respected colleague reports to you that he held a séance in his own home. During the course of the séance, one of the sitters asked if the medium could materialize a sunflower. Following this request, a sunflower, six feet high, fell upon the table. Your colleague produces affidavits from witnesses, each of whom is a respected and honorable man. He insists that both the

house and the medium were carefully examined prior to the séance
and that all precautions were taken to prevent trickery. Further-
more, he concludes that the medium somehow had access to a new
force, one that he refers to as a "psychic force."[5]

Colleagues of Alfred Russell Wallace, the co-founder with
Charles Darwin of the theory of evolution by natural selection,
actually confronted exactly this claim in 1869. Wallace witnessed
the séance, he had the sunflower, fully six feet long, and, he
insisted, he could prove the conditions of the experiment were
impervious to cheating, no matter how skilled the magician.

Until that time, Wallace's colleagues had assumed he shared
their materialistic and naturalistic philosophy. They reacted with
shock, hostility, misinterpretation of his claims, and embarrass-
ment. Darwin himself refused even to discuss Wallace's conver-
sion to spiritualism. Psychologist William B. Carpenter asserted
what some skeptics today still believe; since parapsychology is
impossible, any so-called experimental success must be due either
to deliberate fraud or self-delusion:

> I have no other "theory" to support than that of the constancy of
> the well-ascertained Laws of Nature; and my contention is that
> where apparent departures from them take place through Human
> instrumentality, we are justified in assuming in the first instance
> either *fraudulent* description or unintentional *self-*deception, or
> both combined,—until the absence of either shall have been
> proved by every conceivable test that the sagacity of skeptical
> experts can devise.

Carpenter saw psychic claims as part of an "epidemic delusion"
responsible scientists such as himself were duty-bound to eradi-
cate:

> I have no other motive than a desire to do what I can to save from
> this new form of Epidemic Delusion some who are in danger of
> being smitten by its poison, and to afford to such as desire to keep
> themselves clear from it, a justification for their "common sense"

rejection of testimony pressed upon them by friends whose honesty
they would not for a moment call into question.

Contemporary skeptics echo this complaint too. According to
Paul Kurtz, the founder of the Committee for the Scientific
Investigation of Claims of the Paranormal (CSICOP), wide-
spread belief in the paranormal is symptomatic of an "epidemic
of irrationality." Kurtz points to the Reverend Jim Jones's suicidal
People's Temple as an example of belief in the paranormal leading
to fascism.

Wallace and Carpenter were not arguing science, of course.
Their disagreement was over belief systems, over just what consti-
tutes the "Laws of Nature." Carpenter's mechanistic and materialistic belief system excluded the spiritual; Wallace's belief system
did not. Likewise, both Kurtz and Randi probably reject parapsychology as a matter of principle, although they would claim to be
open-minded.

As often as not, profound differences in belief systems like
these underlie accusations of fraud in parapsychology research.
Both attacks on and defenses of parapsychology are as often as not
attempts to justify the speaker's underlying belief system.

What should be discussed, as Hyman points out in his article
on Wallace, is *factual claims,* and such a discussion requires that
parapsychologists be given a hearing. The relevant question, then,
is what are the conditions under which we must accept an ob-
servation as factual and reject propositions that contradict
them?

Mainstream science has missed important discoveries before
because the community rejected observations later proved factual:
Jefferson's stones from the sky, the theory of contagion Semmel-
weis observed in childbed fever, and even death by voodoo spell.

W. B. Cannon, the discoverer of homeostasis (the state of
physiological equilibrium produced by a proper chemical balance
in an organism), once reported observing murder by magic spell.
Scientists ignored Cannon's report until biologists discovered that

chemicals the body produces in reaction to fear kill laboratory rats.

One of the conditions parapsychologists need to meet is the presence or at least the advice of trained magicians in designing their experiments, as the Parapsychology Association recently recommended. Until the parapsychology community overcomes its reluctance to do so, many of its proofs will not deserve serious consideration.

The skeptical community, in turn, needs to give fair hearing in its forums and journals to parapsychologists who respond fairly to scientific objections to their methodology. Randi, for one, says he would be happy to cooperate: "With proper controls, the parapsychologists won't have any successes to report."

Of course, it is reasonable for the scientific community to maintain that certain of its conclusions are beyond reasonable criticism. In fact, it is necessary to do so. Resources are limited; the United States can't waste research money investigating whether or not the earth is flat, although there is an active Flat Earth Society whose members challenge the scientific consensus. Creationism, the theory that life arose through sudden creation roughly six to ten thousand years ago, is similarly shunned, although there is very wide public support for this hypothesis. Bills have been introduced in the legislatures of thirty-six states mandating the teaching of both creationism and evolution, and the threat of boycott has forced publishers to drop references to evolution in most textbooks.

There are probably more people in the United States willing to exclude poltergeists and reincarnation from research funding than creationism. Creationists have at least masqueraded as scientific, but it is easier to speak of "scientific creationism" than "scientific poltergeists" or "scientific reincarnation," and that difficulty is at the root of the rejection of parapsychologists—they can't get away from connotations of the supernatural.

NOTES

1. *Uri,* by Andrija Puharich, Bantam Books, 1974, p. 220.
2. Quoted in *The Search for Superman,* by John Wilhelm.
3. Puthoff and Targ, *Mind Reach,* p. x.
4. Reprinted by permission from the *Zetetic Scholar,* No. 6, p. 95 (1981).
5. Reprinted by permission from the *Zetetic Scholar,* No. 7 (1981).

5 · PROJECT SCANATE

I⊤ ought to be possible to test the psychics' claims.

Do or die—either psychics can penetrate the world's most closely guarded secrets, or they can't. The CIA, like police agencies, needs results, reliable information, information that can be acted upon. Theory really doesn't matter; how it's done doesn't matter. What matters is the results.

In May 1973, Harold Puthoff and Russell Targ challenged the skeptics with just such a test: psychics versus the CIA, extrasensory perception against the most sophisticated codes known to the U.S. National Security Agency, remote viewing against satellite photography and top U.S. agents behind the iron curtain—the whole of the U.S. national security apparatus cooperating to make cheating impossible.

The test was dubbed "Project Scanate"—an impossible test with impossible results . . .

Puthoff, Targ, and the psychics won.

"What's a nice physicist like you doing in a research area like this?" friends asked Harold Puthoff when he abandoned laser physics for parapsychology. Nothing in his scientific background suggests a propensity to the weird. Behind Puthoff's black hair and youthful face lurks a calculating mind and unflappable temperament.

Harold Puthoff, born June 20, 1936, got his B.S. and M.S. in electrical engineering from the University of Florida, where he was honored as an "outstanding engineering student," and his Ph.D. from Stanford. After graduation, he served in the navy on duty with the National Security Agency at Fort Meade, Maryland.

The National Security Agency (NSA) is the branch of the U.S. intelligence community that intercepts and decrypts foreign communications and codes. The agency is nothing if not more fiercely secretive than even the CIA. Almost never does unauthorized information find its way from NSA to the press; by comparison, the CIA practically advertises its secrets. NSA has the world's largest installation of modern computers, with which technicians attempt to break sophisticated Soviet codes. Puthoff worked as an engineer for Project Light, a top secret study of the applications of esoteric technologies like fiber optics and lasers to high-speed computers. The agency awarded Puthoff a "certificate of commendation for outstanding achievement."

After leaving NSA, Puthoff quickly made his mark in physics with the invention of a tunable, infrared laser. In 1969, he published (in English, French and Russian) *Fundamentals of Quantum Electronics,* now a standard text in the field, and he is listed in *American Men and Women in Science* and in *Who's Who in the West.*

Puthoff's partner in the Scanate tests, Russell Targ, does not have such impressive academic credentials, but his work with gas lasers is well respected. Targ is tall, with wild blond hair, a quick temper, and the same nervous distrust of the press as his brother-in-law, former world chess champion Bobby Fisher.

Stanford Research Institute, where Puthoff and Targ conducted the Scanate tests, is located in Menlo Park, California. The institute was founded in 1946 as a wholly owned subsidiary of Stanford University and became independent in 1970, after student and faculty protests over the institute's heavy involvement in military research. The government funds 75 percent of the institute's research; 40 percent of that funding comes from the Pentagon.

SRI researches almost anything, as long as the client fits its no-nonsense, conservative reputation and, more importantly, as long as the price is right. SRI's top-notch scientists do not come cheap, but they've earned their reputation for accomplishment. SRI designed the funny computer-readable numbers on checks, recommended the Orlando location for Disney World, and analyzed the eighteen-minute gap on a Watergate tape for Richard Nixon. Under contract to the army, SRI chemists studied psychoactive compounds like LSD for their potential as chemical-warfare agents. Its biologists tested seals and sea lions, hoping to discover new means of underwater communication for the navy.

Puthoff secured private backing for his initial experiments—all SRI researchers arrange their own funding—from San Antonio fried chicken franchiser Bill Church, whose Science Unlimited Research Foundation (SURF) funds everything from solar-energy projects to exotic attempts to contact extraterrestrials. Puthoff signed a contract with SRI and hired Russell Targ as a full-time assistant for psychic research.

Puthoff first proposed research in psychic phenomena to SRI in 1972, while the institute was handling a laser patent for him. A copy of Puthoff's proposal reached Clive Backster, the polygraph operator who claimed he could measure the emotions of plants. Backster showed the proposal to an associate, painter and psychic Ingo Swann. Swann wrote Puthoff, volunteering to participate in his experiments.

Swann is tall, a bit pudgy, and seldom without a cigar. Today he lives quietly in Greenwich Village, paints, and now prefers to avoid the notoriety of the psychic circuit, although he does participate in some unpublicized research.

In 1973, when Puthoff and Targ began their psychic studies, Swann made his living as a psychic. Nevertheless, by Puthoff's account, the first test he proposed "shocked and dismayed"[1] even the professional. Puthoff asked Swann to alter the signal from SRI's magnetometer, a sensitive device used to measure magnetism and theoretically shielded from any possibility of tampering by a formidable array of safeguards. The device is buried in an eight-ton iron vault set in concrete under the floor and shielded from stray magnetism by a copper coil, an aluminum container, a smaller copper container, and finally a supercooled electrical coil —by all appearances, an impregnable device and an impossible test.

Swann's "state of shock propelled him into a sufficiently altered state of consciousness" to succeed in the impossible.[2] After five seconds of concentration, the device's ink trace wavered. The startled observers asked Swann if he could stop the trace altogether, and five seconds later, the trace abruptly stopped.

The next tests with Swann were more conventional, but with what Puthoff calls "high-tech twists." Instead of guessing whether an experimenter had selected a red or a green card, one of the standard menu of ESP card tests, Swann guessed whether a red helium-neon or a green argon laser in another room was on.

The blinking lasers didn't keep Swann entertained for long. Swann got bored; lasers or no, such conventional tests "trivialized" his abilities.

"Why don't we do something exciting?" he suggested.

Swann had participated in remote-viewing tests at the American Society for Psychical Research in New York with "significant" results, according to the researchers there. Exciting tests? You bet; Swann claimed he could send his mind anywhere in the world, and even to other planets, and describe what was there. All he needed was coordinates like the latitude and longitude—"Let's design an experiment around that!"

Scanate, "scan by coordinate," was born.

According to Puthoff and Targ, a man from the government "heard we were doing ESP experiments" and casually dropped by SRI. The government visitor came from an agency Puthoff and Targ refer to cryptically as "our East Coast challenger." He remains nameless, referred to only as visitor 1, "V1."

He wanted "to see something psychic."

One can safely guess that the visit was much less casual than the scientists suggest. The East Coast challenger was the CIA, and V1 was a case officer assigned to monitor psychic research.

Puthoff and Targ don't like to talk about the intelligence community; sometimes they have even gone so far as to feign ignorance of the CIA connection.

But V1, whom I interviewed on condition I not reveal his name, says the scientists not only knew his employer but solicited the visit. Both the CIA and SRI itself discourage publicity, especially when the research is both classified and controversial, but Puthoff and Targ's coyness about government interest in their work seems excessive. An investigative reporter or even a casual reader need not be psychic to divine the identity of their East Coast challenger.

In 1973, the CIA had assigned half a dozen agents to canvass parapsychology laboratories for new technologies that might have military or intelligence applications. Uri Geller particularly interested the CIA, and agents discreetly attended his performances. If Geller's mind could bend utensils and start broken watches, he might also be able to affect computers, the agency reasoned, and much of the intelligence business today depends on computers.

It seems unlikely that neither Puthoff nor Targ nor the SRI management was aware of government interest in psychic phenomena or Uri Geller. New ventures like psychic research, especially when their disclosure might affect SRI's conservative reputation, require special approval. Puthoff and Targ got that approval, and it's doubtful that they based their application on the hope of continued largess from fried chicken tycoon Bill Church.

The moment SRI approved the project and Bill Church's SURF had provided intitial funding, Targ set out on a nationwide tour to secure government funding for more extensive tests. Puthoff and Targ also brought Geller, whose supposed powers already intrigued the CIA, to SRI for extensive tests.

Which agencies did Targ solicit? Puthoff, Targ, and SRI management refuse to be specific. "Any agency at all," says Targ.

In fact, most of the agencies were military, and SRI eventually got funding from both the navy and the CIA. NASA, the space agency, and ARPA, the Pentagon's Advanced Research Projects Agency, seriously reviewed SRI proposals. NASA eventually sponsored a small project, while ARPA, for reasons already discussed, withdrew.

V1, who wanted "to see something psychic," had reason not to be entirely skeptical. Years before, he had saved the life of a foreign agent, either through an incredible stroke of luck or just perhaps, he thought, through a psychic intuition.

In the mid-fifties, V1 worked as a CIA case officer in West Germany. Case officers recruit and maintain liaison with spies; V1 worked primarily with Soviet and Eastern bloc military personnel who for one reason or another had agreed to cooperate with the CIA.

One of those spies, a Hungarian general in West Germany to buy a Mercedes, had been discovered. Unknown to the general, the secret police waited for him at the border. V1 was ordered to warn the general.

The agency knew he had picked up the car in the German city of Strasburg earlier that day and assumed he would stay overnight before driving to the border. V1's mission sounds easy, but there was a catch. For reasons he still can't reveal, his orders were to find the general *without notifying any German authorities.* He didn't even reach the city until two in the morning.

How do you find an individual in a city of more than a million souls, an individual unlikely even to be registered under his true name, at two in the morning, and without notifying anyone in authority? V1 had no better idea than you or I.

As he approached the city on the autobahn, V1 saw a Mercedes advertising sign high on a building. With nothing better to do, he drove to the sign. He found a darkened office building on a square. Despondently, V1 crossed the street to his parked car. He stopped; he noticed a small alley. Parked in the alley was a Mercedes, a *new* Mercedes. Near the Mercedes he saw the door of a small inn.

There was no reason to suppose that Mercedes belonged to the general, and no reason to suppose the general had gone to that inn, and no reason to suppose that if by the wildest stroke of luck the general did stay there, his room was at the top of the stairs. V1 went directly to that room and knocked on the door. The general answered.

V1 told the general what awaited him at home and offered political asylum in the United States. The general, obviously relieved and astonished, asked how he had been found. Certainly no less astonished himself, V1 still had the aplomb to reply that the agency keeps a more careful watch over its own than the general imagined.

Despite the odds, twenty years later V1 remained as willing to credit dumb luck as parapsychology. He approached Puthoff and Targ skeptically.

"One of the things we learned quickly in our new program," according to Puthoff and Targ, "is that no matter how miraculous the result of an ESP demonstration, an observer often tries to discount it as a lucky day . . . in a word, the only way to be sure the observer has seen something psychic is to have him do [the psychic feat] himself."[3]

V1 agreed to be the viewer in a remote-viewing test. While Targ and he waited in a comfortable lounge, Puthoff went to a target site selected at random by a neutral party. At the appointed time, V1 recorded his impressions on a cassette, describing a wooden walkway with a railing and the ground falling away underneath. That description obviously matched the target, a footbridge over a stream in nearby Burgess Park.

An impressive demonstration, but V1 the skeptic wasn't convinced. Perhaps Targ had given him unconscious cues. He wanted to be alone with the tape recorder, and sat in a corner with his hands over his ears and his eyes shut.

Despite those precautions, he did even better on the second test, correctly describing the triangular ribs and electrical shielding of a TV transmission tower along with an adjacent small movie theater.

Convinced? Not yet, demurred V1. Perhaps Puthoff had listened to the tape and then selected a corresponding target. For the third test, V1 sat alone with his eyes shut and his ears covered, and both he and the team at the site made recordings and sketches. The sketches and recordings were exchanged before anyone said anything.

This time, V1 had to concede, "My God, it really works." His taped impressions and drawings obviously depicted the target, a playground merry-go-round four miles from SRI.

The precautions V1 took might seem proof against any fraud, but Puthoff and Targ can with some justification claim the really Draconian precautions for the official test V1 proposed made Scanate "the most severely monitored scientific experiment in history." CIA headquarters personnel would select a pool of potential targets all over the world, including secret sites in the United States, the Soviet Union, and the People's Republic of China. Another headquarters group would, without the knowledge of the first, randomly select the targets actually used from that pool. The National Security Agency would then encrypt the coordinates and transmit them, in code, to V1 and other agency personnel assigned to monitor Scanate at SRI. No one outside the headquarters, including V1, knew which targets were selected.

In some cases, Puthoff and Targ's psychics couldn't cheat even if they had known the targets. The CIA deliberately selected sites in the Soviet Union and China scheduled for satellite surveillance two or three months after the test. Until those satellite photos came in, no one in the United States could know what to expect. Other sites were inaccessible even to the satellites—inside build-

ings at Soviet bases or in areas not covered by any spy satellite—
but were scheduled for "ground truth checks" by U.S. in-country
agents. Finally, V1 proposed showing the psychics photographs
of Soviet and U.S. submarines and asking exactly where they
would be at a given time. Just the photograph—even though
thirty or forty vessels of the same class may be identical. The
Soviets randomly change even the numbers on the sides of their
ships, so the few photos on which hull numbers were visible would
be of no help, even if you assumed that Ingo Swann and the other
psychics tested knew the hull number, name, and planned route
of every ship in the Soviet navy. U.S. Navy intelligence personnel
were assigned to monitor this portion of the tests.

Scanate began in May 1973. Testing continued for two years.

Puthoff and Targ agreed to V1's conditions for the tests. The
next step was to get more psychic subjects.

Volunteers came eagerly: Duane Elgin, a young SRI social
scientist and futurist (a person who tries to predict future patterns
of social evolution), Hella Hammid, a free-lance photographer,
Marshall Pease and Phyllis Cole, two SRI staffers. Richard Bach,
author of *Jonathan Livingston Seagull*, joined in 1974. Unlike
Swann, none had significant experience as a psychic.

Puthoff and Targ got dozens of calls every month from would-
be psychics who had heard of their ESP research, if not the CIA
connection. They tried to explain to callers that since everyone
seems to have latent remote-viewing abilities, SRI could not test
everyone.

One caller tried out for the team. On June 1, 1973, Pat Price,
a businessman and former police commissioner of Burbank, California, called Puthoff. Price claimed that he had used his pychic
abilities as police commissioner "to track down suspects."

On impulse, Puthoff gave Price the coordinates for the latest
series of targets selected by the CIA, including an area in Virginia
approximately 135 miles southwest of Washington, D.C. Three
days later, he got Price's five-page written response in the mail,

"beginning with a description of the area from an altitude of 1,500 feet and ending with a tour through building interiors. The tour was complete with descriptions of equipment, names from desks, and—just to show he was serious—a list of a dozen labelings on file folders locked in a file cabinet."[4]

Price said he "mashed [his] head" into that file cabinet, and "felt" the labels:

Cue Ball
Four Ball
Eight Ball
Fourteen Ball
Rackup
Side Pocket

All terms from the game of pool, seemingly meaningless in labyrinthian buildings of "underground storage areas," and communications and computer equipment manned by Army Signal Corps personnel, according to Price.

Puthoff forwarded Price's response to the "East Coast challenger," confident, he says, that such a detailed description of an alleged secret military installation couldn't be right.

Three weeks later, the CIA informed him that Price was right. Exactly right.

And not only Price. Swann correctly described a previously unknown Soviet installation, sketching buildings and rail lines, and noting an "unusually high proportion of women" among the personnel. A U.S. spy satellite verified Swann's report three months later.

Given the coordinates latitude 49 degrees 20' south, longitude 70 degrees 14' east, and asked to respond immediately without the use of a map, Swann answered:

My initial response is that it's an island, maybe a mountain sticking up through cloud cover. Terrain seems rocky. . . . Very cold. I see some buildings rather mathematically laid out. One of them is orange. Two white cylindrical tanks, quite large. . . .[5]

Swann went on to describe the joint Soviet/French weather research station on the antarctic island of Kerguelen, right down to the outhouse.

Not all Swann's responses hit the target with such detail, but time after time, his descriptions were obviously inspired. Given latitude 45 degrees north, longitude 150 degrees west, he correctly responded "ocean." Latitude 2 degrees south, longitude 34 degrees east, the eastern shore of Lake Victoria in Africa, elicited "sense of speeding over water, landing on land, lake to west, high elevation." A few responses were ambiguous, like "open water, stands of pine to north" for a point in Canada's Hudson Bay. Swann recorded one miss in this series of ten tests; given coordinates for the Sea of Okhotsk, he responded doubtfully, "not many trees, patches of snow, marsh?"

Other volunteers correctly predicted Soviet and U.S. submarine movements after seeing an unlabeled photograph of the target vessel, penetrated meetings held inside the CIA headquarters, and claimed to penetrate similar meetings behind the iron curtain.

The agency commissioned an independent evaluation of the Scanate tests from intelligence consultant Joseph A. Ball of Santa Barbara, California. Ball concluded that Scanate "produced manifestations of extrasensory perception sufficiently sharp and clear-cut to justify serious considerations of possible applications."

Ball cautioned that "practical applications" of remote viewing, that is, psychic spying, would never replace traditional intelligence techniques:

No matter how gifted the paragnost [psychic], existing ignorance of the basis of paranormal phenomena together with the capricious and unreliable nature of the channel dictate that information derived from this source can never stand alone and must be used with caution. Extrasensory information should *at best* supplement normal information or guide its collection, but should never serve in place of it.[6]

Another consulting contract, finished a year later, reached the same conclusions: "It is our considered opinion that it is worthwhile for the United States government to initiate and support systematic research in this area." The CIA paid the AiResearch Manufacturing Company of Torrence, California, one hundred thousand dollars for the study, prepared by an interdisciplinary research team including a psychologist, a physicist, a signal enhancement expert, and an instrumentation engineer. That study also considered Soviet research. The authors even mimicked the Soviets in one respect; they substituted good technical gobbledygook for occult-sounding terms like *ESP* and *psychic*. Both the title of the AiResearch report, "Novel Biological Information Transfer Mechanisms (NBIT)," and the text, which does not once mention the words *extrasensory* or *psychic*, would warm the hearts of materialist Marxist philosophers (and some pennypinching American bureaucrats who aren't Marxist). Interestingly, the researchers reported no Soviet interest in remote viewing.

Nineteen seventy-six was also the first time that parapsychology research got direct and enthusiastic support from the CIA director, then George Bush. Bush was approached by Edgar Mitchell, a personal friend for many years. Mitchell's Institute for Noetic [from the Greek word meaning "new"] Sciences in San Francisco, which he founded to promote psychic research, had worked closely with Puthoff and Targ at SRI. Bush gave Mitchell permission to organize high-level seminars at the CIA to discuss possible intelligence applications of parapsychology.

Despite all this support, parapsychology research never got institutionalized at the CIA. Scattered research projects continue to this day, but no central office for psychic research coordinates it. Parapsychology information does not even supplement routine intelligence estimates, as recommended by the consulting reports, except in rare and extraordinary instances.

One reason is that in 1977 the director changed. Adm. Stansfield Turner, the Carter appointee, had no personal interest in the subject.

Edgar Mitchell blames the problems on simple bureaucratic inertia. "We just couldn't get the actors together," said Mitchell, "there was always one bureaucratic bottleneck or another."

There were also, and still are, dedicated skeptics at the agency, people who opposed even the most modest investment in psychic research on principle. Mitchell has nothing but scorn for the skeptics: "There are still people who don't believe I went to the moon. Some people just won't listen to reason."

The primary objection to the practical application of parapsychology, however, was reliability. "Do you want to risk lives on this stuff?" co-workers asked V1. Even Scanate's star performers, Ingo Swann and Pat Price, expressed doubts about the reliability of their abilities. "Several breakthroughs [are] needed to uncover the remote-viewing possibilities," said Swann, noting that even his obviously inspired responses often included some inaccurate information:

> Accumulated responses from subjects' attempts to view distant targets indicate that the target is often actually viewed, but in some way the target also acts as a prompter for the spontaneous appearance of seemingly irrelevant data . . . it seems reasonable to assume that we are dealing with automatic analytic functions of some sort, and that, hypothetically, these are the source of the diluted or erroneous information.[7]

Price, the amateur psychic, dealt with his limitations more impishly, asking secretaries, "If I can see anywhere in the universe, why would I want to follow you to the bathroom?"

Armed with the classified Scanate reports, Puthoff, Targ, and V1 visited dozens of government agencies hoping to fund further research outside the CIA.

The navy signed a $50,703 contract to determine whether psychics could detect remote electromagnetic sources. If psychics can sense a flashing light in another room, perhaps they could also detect the very weak electromagnetic emanations from submerged submarines.

SRI delivered the final report for this contract in 1978, claiming success with Swann, Price, Uri Geller, and others. The navy isn't bragging about their apparent success. In response to congressional inquiries about the contract in 1982, navy spokesmen refused to characterize the study as psychic, calling it an "investigation of the apparent ability of certain individuals to detect remote electromagnetic signals at a noncognitive level of awareness."

Targ calls this contract "a milestone" because, "for the first time, we had physiological correlates [EEG traces] to the psychic performance." Critics of the experiments, which are unclassified, say the researchers were guilty of "optimal stopping," which means quitting while you're ahead. An independent evaluation commissioned by the navy was noncommittal as to the scientific value of the tests, but exonerated the researchers of any alleged chicanery.

Puthoff, who reviewed this manuscript, counters that "the 'optimal stopping' criticism [stopping while ahead] couldn't possibly [rationally] have been leveled at this experiment, because we didn't 'quit while ahead'; the final series went in the opposite direction and made the results difficult to interpret . . . just the opposite of optimal stopping."

In 1976, the navy signed another contract with SRI, this one for $26,000, to find out if psychics could influence magnetometers; it was SRI's heavily shielded research magnetometer, remember, on which Puthoff first tested Ingo Swann's powers. The navy uses mobile versions of these devices to detect the magne-tism of submerged substances.

"The navy has a vital interest in anything that can influence these devices," stated Dr. Joel Lawson. At that time, Lawson headed the Naval Electronic Systems Command, which spon-sored all three projects. Until he was officially silenced, Lawson was one of the very few navy officials willing to discuss psychic warfare openly. "I have always believed," he admitted, "that ESP is the only way to fight submarines. The magnetometer tests were designed to prove the principle."

The navy electronics research facility in San Diego also signed a contract to study the influence of extremely low frequency (ELF) electromagnetic radiation of the human mind. Soviet re-searchers theorize these radiations might be the vehicle for ESP communication and have tried to construct "remote physiological monitors" to measure persons' vital signs and mood at a distance.

The navy is interested in ELF because it plans to bury hun-dreds of miles of cable in Wisconsin. The plan, Project Seafarer (formerly Project Sanguine), has enraged environmentalists and local citizens who fear that ELF radiation may affect people's health. The navy has steadfastly claimed ELF radiation does not affect humans, conveniently ignoring its own study of "ELF and Mind Control."

Outside the navy and the CIA, however, SRI had few takers. NASA paid thirty-five-thousand dollars for an "ESP teaching machine" designed by SRI and University of California psi re-searcher Charles Tart, but the Defense Advanced Research Proj-ects Agency twice refused to fund research after on-site evalua-tions of Puthoff and Targ's work. The air force, already funding its own independent parapsychology research, had no interest in remote-viewing studies.

The bottom line, however, as Targ points out, is that the government has supported SRI's psychic research for a decade and continues to do so. "Few projects," says Targ, "have maintained that sort of support. The reason we [Puthoff and Targ] got it is because our work produced credible results."

With such impressive controls, the most stringent bars to fraud our intelligence agencies could devise, it may be somewhat surprising that Puthoff and Targ were nevertheless widely suspected of cheating. These suspicions, rather than any defect in the Scanate report, dissuaded several potential sponsors of SRI's research.

In contrast to these days of tight budgets, in 1975 agencies were actually anxious to fund psychic research. An internal CIA memo frankly admitted, "Public interest in psi phenomena has been on the upswing since 1975," and the time was therefore opportune for such research within the CIA. DARPA's director, Dr. George Lawrence, was ordered by his superiors to find something to satisfy congressional demands to match purported Soviet efforts in the field. The congressmen, with the exception of the few like Charlie Rose with a special interest in the field, were responding to the mail from their constituents. Skeptics within agencies simply couldn't suppress such intense public interest. In the absence of some disturbing hint of fraud, scientists with the reputation and organizational backing Puthoff and Targ commanded should have been buried in work.

Unfortunately, there was a hint of intrigue hanging over Puthoff and Targ in 1975 . . . an unfair hint, certainly, that had nothing to do with their competency as scientists or the design of the experiments.

The hint involved religion—or a cult, depending on your point of view. Three of the project members, Puthoff, Swann, and Price, had at one time or another taken courses offered by the Church—some would say, the cult—of Scientology, although none were directly involved in the church.

Scientology is the brainstorm of science-fiction writer L. Ron Hubbard, an offshoot of the mental- and physical-health regimen he recommended in his little yellow book, *Dianetics: The Modern Science of Mental Health,* in the early fifties. Today,

Scientology claims three million members recruited through its missions.

In 1978, the FBI uncovered an extensive Scientology plot to infiltrate, spy on, and harass government agencies investigating their affairs. Federal raids on their headquarters also turned up documentation of "Operation PC Freak Out," an attempt to discredit a free-lance journalist investigating the church's methods.

No one suspected the Scientologists of spying on the federal government in 1975, when Puthoff and Targ were canvassing for additional funding, but rumors about the church scared off at least four potential sponsors.

Puthoff says his involvement with the church more than a decade ago was casual and Targ, who is not a Scientologist, vehemently rejects any allegation that the church could influence *his* research.

Science correspondent John Wilhelm first hinted at the possibility of a connection between Scientologist espionage and the success of Scanate in the *Washington Post* on August 7, 1977. Wilhelm had published *The Search for Superman* a year earlier. "The purpose" of the book, Wilhelm stated in the introduction, "is to present the facts as best they can be determined in the controversial psychic experiments carried out in the past several years at Stanford Research Institute. My intent is to neither prove nor disprove the widely disputed claims . . . rather, it is an inquiry into the specifics of such claims."

He found a new reality in the remote-viewing experiments with Price and Swann. "Is it so outrageous," he asked his readers, "to suggest that the top of the evolutionary ladder, Homo sapiens, might have undiscovered modes of sensing?" For himself, the answer was no. "Barring fraud, I am persuaded that extended vision does take place."

Barring fraud? Wilhelm trusted the researchers: "Puthoff and Targ are men of good faith, and despite the large number of Scientologists involved in the SRI research, I found no evidence that any covert conspiracy attempted to subvert or bias their results."

When he published his *Washington Post* piece, Wilhelm had started to have doubts. Publicly, Wilhelm suggested, but never flatly claimed, chicanery in SRI's experiments.

When I first began to write this book, I frankly thought the evidence of fraud so self-evident I didn't spend too much time looking into the charges. I intended to entitle this chapter "Cash Reach: Scientists Look at Pentagon Funding" in parody of Puthoff's and Targ's book, *Mind Reach: Scientists Look at Psychic Ability.* I did, and still do, find remote viewing as accurate as that claimed for Swann and Price so fantastic as to be ridiculous. I may be wrong, but, to quote one eminent physicist who read SRI's report, "This is something I won't believe even if it turns out to be true." I personally might never accept the reality of remote viewing, no matter how overwhelming the evidence.

Mine would not have been the first such public allegation. What Wilhelm hinted about Scanate in the *Washington Post,* others stated flatly about an SRI contract with NASA for an ESP teaching machine. I believed these allegations too, but fortunately, Puthoff persuaded me to investigate. I did, and I found the allegations were simply not true. There is no evidence whatsoever that Puthoff and Targ or any of their subjects cheated on this contract; there is evidence some of the allegations against Puthoff and Targ were deliberately fabricated to discredit psychic research. NASA officials who supposedly uncovered the cheating vouched for the integrity of the experiments, although for one reason or another they were unconvinced that the tests had any scientific value.

Personally, I cannot accept the reality of remote viewing, and yet have no evidence of fraud. Even if there were such evidence, isn't to suggest that an outfit like the Church of Scientology could have penetrated the national security community to the extent necessary to defeat the Scanate protocols just as outrageous as to suggest undiscovered modes of sensing at the top of the evolutionary ladder?

When you eliminate the impossible, whatever is left must be true . . . except in this case, everything seems impossible.

Puthoff and Targ are reluctant to talk directly about the military implications of remote viewing. Their book, *Mind Reach*, not only evades the subject with rather obvious circumlocutions like "East Coast challenger" and "government visitor," but contains outright contradictions. For example, an introduction by anthropologist Margaret Mead states:

> An issue, which will undoubtedly be picked up by the sensationist press, and which flows from the accounts of Soviet interest in mind influencing from a distance, is the prevalence of fantasies surrounding spying and being spied upon. "Could the enemy read the President's mind?" as one newspaper account put it. But such fantasies of omnipotence or total vulnerability to inimical forces have been continuously fed and exaggerated for over a quarter of a century by the science fiction in which many dilemmas are solved, not by science, but by ESP. These fictions represent easy solutions, most likely unreal and certainly regressive and unchallenging in nature.[8]

This invective introduces a book about tests designed primarily to demonstrate to the CIA the validity of psychic spying. No matter, it is followed by Richard Bach's foreword, which has this to say about such fantasies of omnipotence or vulnerability to inimical forces:

> When I first realized the implications of the Targ/Puthoff research, I was afraid for their lives—these were established scientists who had found a principle that has made secrets impossible. But it is now too late to burn the files; what they've done is already being duplicated and expanded in laboratories around the world.[9]

One shouldn't infer from such contradictions that Puthoff and Targ are deliberately obfuscating. As I know only too well from personal experience, persons caught in a malestrom of controversy can't avoid making statements that seem contradictory in cold print. Usually, the apparent contradictions result from changes of emphasis, making one point about the facts on one occasion and a slightly different but legitimate point on another. People shouldn't be expected to speak, or even write, as if they were preparing a lawyer's brief.

The government's few public statements on the Scanate tests are just as rife with contradictions. For the most part, spokesmen simply refuse to concede any interest in psychic research, anytime, anywhere. Occasionally, they express "limited interest in what the Soviets might be doing," and rarely an official like the navy's Lawson calls parapsychology a "vital interest." Faced with copies of the contracts, the navy just flat out lies—standard operating procedure, I have learned over the years. No organization in the government cooperates less with the press.

John Wilhelm had no better luck with the navy than I. He obtained a copy of the top secret Scanate report, including the coordinates of the top secret installation whose files Pat Price allegedly read. He drove to the site, "half expecting to discover the base camp of an extraterrestrial scouting party or, at the very least, the command center for World War III." What he found was another one of those exasperating ambiguities—

A sparse hillside, a few flocks of sheep, and lots of droppings. No "underground storage areas," no "computers, communication equipment" or "Army Signal Corps" personnel, as reported by Price. The only code word was the name of the place, Bullpasture Mountain. Under the circumstances, it seems SRI's "Project Scanate" would be named more appropriately "Project Bullpasture."

When told of the results of [my] hike, James Foote, the Navy project manager for the SRI tests, was astonished: "I am just chagrined we didn't catch this. . . . There's definitely some fallacy in this Scanate report."

Several days later, Foote abruptly changed his tune. After checking with his contacts "across the river," he reversed himself completely: "From what I have seen it was a valid test as far as the investigators are concerned." The excuses range from: (1) the NSA or CIA man "couldn't read the map" and therefore the coordinates got confused; and/or (2) the psychic subjects zoomed in on the nearby Sugar Grove space communications center (which does have similarities to the described target, but is in West Virginia, has public tours through it and so is not secret, and is manned by Navy, not Army, personnel; and/or (3) the subjects read the mind of the NSA officer rather than the coordinates. Says Foote: "There may have been slight exaggeration, but it was a matter of degree rather than a deliberate falsehood." (*Washington Post*, August 7, 1977, page B1.)

Publicly, Wilhelm has never stated his conclusions from all this contradictory evidence—evidence that could indicate fraud, confusion, or simply sloppy record keeping.

Puthoff told the author he did not know whether the file labels, "Four Ball," "Rackup," and the others, are really top secret code words. V1 and two other sources confirmed the codes. Price certainly zoomed in on some secrets, and his description does fit an area at NSA's Fort Meade, Maryland, headquarters. In addition, the subjects zeroed in on hundreds of coordinates, not just the mysterious communication center, and indisputably got most of them right. Those successes can't all be written off as recording errors. The experiments make a case, however controversial, for the reality of remote viewing.

According to former Reagan White House aide Barbara Honegger, the National Security Agency is testing remote viewing on NSA's primary job, breaking codes. Even NSA's acres of computers are often overwhelmed by the trillions of combinations needed to crack sophisticated Soviet codes. If psychic enhancement of the computer reduces the workload by even one tenth of one percent, trillions become billions—still formidable, but feasible for high-speed computers.

Targ has recently left SRI and is working independently on psychotronics and dowsing. Puthoff and Ingo Swann are reportedly continuing their work in "applied remote viewing" for the navy and the CIA.

Adm. Stansfield Turner remained skeptical about the possibility of remote viewing. At a breakfast for journalists in 1977, referring to the CIA's experiments with Pat Price, Turner said only that the CIA "had an individual who from time to time was able to draw very elementary sketches of street scenes in foreign countries where he had not been. Sometimes these sketches had a reasonable relationship to reality." Turner did acknowledge that the CIA strongly suspected that the Soviets had done a fair amount of research into parapsychology. The CIA ended its own experiments with Pat Price in 1975—"He died," said Turner drily, "and we haven't heard from him since."

NOTES

1. *Mind Reach,* by Harold Puthoff and Russell Targ, Delta Books, 1977, p. 21.
2. Ibid., p. 21.
3. Ibid., p. 6.
4. Ibid., p. 48
5. Ibid., p. 31
6. John Wilhelm, "Psychic Spying?", *Washington Post,* August 7, 1977, p. 81.
7. Puthoff and Targ, op. cit., p. 41.
8. Ibid., p. xxi.
9. Ibid., p. xxv.

6 · FIRST EARTH BATTALION

PARAPSYCHOLOGISTS are unlikely to gain scientific respectability through their experimental successes, which have been few and open to controversy, like Scanate.

"There are three ways parapsychology might move into the mainstream," according to Marcello Truzzi. "A solid, repeatable experimental demonstration is one way, but no one has come up with such an experiment."

Another route would be a revolutionary new theory in one of the basic mainstream sciences like physics or psychology, a theory that indicates psi must exist. For example, parapsychology experiments in precognition—experiments where the subject correctly identifies a target before it is selected—contradict current physical theories. It is perfectly conceivable that a new theory might allow, or even demand, precognition, although no such theory looms on the horizon.

"The third route to respectability," says Truzzi, "is in vogue—applied psi." Parapsychologists hope to get de facto recognition from the scientific community by moving out of the laboratories and into industry and government, demonstrating that psi can solve problems. California think tanks that used to invite gurus or hold seminars on "LSD and creativity" now send "applied psi" newsletters to industry, police forces, and government agencies. Applied psi, claim the advocates, solves problems, even if no one quite understands how.

In 1979, the army had a problem. Ninety percent of the soldiers who operate and maintain the army's seven thousand nuclear weapons in Europe flunked basic tests of their military skills that year. This is an appalling statistic, but it should come as no surprise. For years, the all-volunteer army had been failing. The army of 1979 was an army of misfits—uneducated, ill-trained, and illiterate. It was an army that, according to its own secret estimates, would "not be taken seriously by our allies or our adversaries."

Two years later, the army still had problems. Seven of its ten U.S.-based combat divisions were rated "not ready for combat" due to personnel problems.

The question facing the modern U.S. Army, experts had concluded at the Pentagon, was not whether its soldiers were unfit, but what to do about it. A growing number of army futurists advocated a really unique solution to the army's dilemma, a miracle cure—the First Earth Battalion.

The year is 1991. Fierce artillery duels mar the truce between Israel and the three-year-old Lebanese unity government. Soviet and American warships maneuver warily fifty miles off the coast.

The United Nations Security Council votes to put a three-thousand-man peace-keeping force between the rivals, but the Central Intelligence Agency predicts war before the force arrives. The president must act now. He must deploy the warrior monks of the First Earth Battalion.

From the First Earth Station in Sante Fe, New Mexico, the first twenty warrior monks wade through a crowd of reporters to a waiting transport. Half are civilians, half military; half men, half women. The youngest is fourteen and the oldest will celebrate his seventy-fifth birthday on the plane; they are one age, new. All are experienced parachutists and possess superior intelligence and the ability to make rational decisions under life-and-death pressure.

During the twelve-hour trip, most place their brains in delta-wave states to conserve energy. A few test their ESP communication channels; others listen to rock music on standard GI cassette recorders.

The warrior monks carry the best equipment modern technology can produce: lightweight laser assault rifles, hallucinogen mortars, amphetamines and night-vision foods, acupuncture kits, dowsing rods for locating hidden tunnels and mines. They are prepared to fight, but they know the force of arms is the weakest power at their disposal. The strongest is the force of love.

Each is sworn to uphold the credo of "high commandos and guerrilla gurus":

I have the capacity and therefore the duty to contribute to the development of myself, my associates, and our planet, simultaneously, now!

I take personal responsibility for generating evolutionary conspiracies as a regular part of my work.

I will select and create conspiratorial mechanisms that are not costly in time or resources because I am aware of the many free channels available to me (such as radio, television, and word of mouth).

I will organize a self-supporting high commando group that will create and perform evolutionary breakthrough actions on behalf of people and planet. One people, one planet.

I will then pass this concept on to others who are capable of generating further self-organizing commando teams.

I will await the time when my group can connect naturally with others at higher and higher levels of awareness and performance— the Natural Guard."

The credo and the First Earth Battalion itself are the brainchild of Lt. Col. Jim Channon, U.S. Army. In 1979, Channon was assigned to investigate the human potential movement for Task Force Delta, an army think tank of officers, futurists, and psychologists formed to study the potential of new technologies to solve the army's then-critical personnel problems. Channon visited more than 130 California groups ranging from Urantia book reading to Tae Kwon Do karate and "est" (Erhard seminar training.)

"California," says Channon, "is ten years ahead of the rest of the country in awareness, thanks to the human potential movement. The army needs to get involved. If we can't offer a policy of hope by the 1990s, we'll be booed out of the country."

Channon's solution was the First Earth Battalion, a conceptual model of the army of the next decade. "Earth and battalion blended perfectly," says Channon, "a union of the natural and action philosophies."

The First Earth Battalion's charter initiation was conducted at the second quarterly meeting of Task Force Delta. The group sat around a table at the Army War College officers' club at Fort Leavenworth, with a candle and a dollar bill at the center. Channon did an acupuncture technique to symbolize their bond to the earth and commitment to help one another realize their goal of a New Age army. A colonel did a karate form. The group chanted a mantra, a word or sound chanted to reach a higher state of consciousness—in this case, a long E for "earth." At first, giggles broke out.

Channon explained the significance of the great seal on the dollar bill and the words *in God we trust:* God is light, truth, love, and evolution. *E Pluribus Unum* describes not one dollar out of many but the "unity of the races."

"Warriors of the spirit," says Channon, "can see many values captured in the most widely communicated piece of printed material in history—the one-dollar bill . . . the pyramid is capped by the spirit eye indicating the order of the ages . . . it is America's role to lead the world to paradise."

Barbara Marx Hubbard, a Delta psychologist, suggested that

the First Earth Battalion could "bombard the Soviets with psychic love rather than hate and suspicion." Task Force Delta
bought the idea, and the First Earth Battalion was born.

The First Earth Battalion intrigued some members of the
army's higher command, but the question of whether or not the
battalion is "official" is open to interpretation. Channon himself
claims he doesn't know, and says "I'm not sure the question is
important." Lt. Col. John Alexander, a friend of Channon, calls
the official status of First Earth "a gray area—a question of who
owns an idea."

Army public affairs statements about the current official status
of the First Earth Battalion tend to ambiguity: "We really don't
know much about it." According to the deputy director of Task
Force Delta, Tom Kelly, "Some people think First Earth is a great
idea, and some people think it's terrible. It's hard to get a consensus."

Channon organized and incorporated the First Earth Battalion
Foundation in Sante Fe, New Mexico, on a wholly private, non-
profit basis, but hopes for government funding "when enough
people have written their congressmen." A dozen candidates and
eighty-one masters have already been selected for the New World
Academy student body and faculty. Plans exist for a "First Earth
Station" command post and "New World City."

Officially, however, the First Earth Battalion is something
more than an idea. Both West Point and the Command and Staff
College include the First Earth Battalion in their human relations
curricula, using a twenty-minute video tape prepared by West
Point. Channon claims more than eight-hundred officers are in
the network that distribute First Earth materials through the
army chain of command. The army has loaned Channon, who
dubs himself "a hack Merlin," to a dozen other government
agencies, including the Los Angeles and Seattle police departments, to explain First Earth concepts, and Channon has received
official permission to speak, in uniform, on television and national

radio featurettes. Until 1980, Channon was assigned to Fort Lewis, near Seattle, where he worked with the "high-technology test bed," a unit designated to test new equipment and ideas, including some developed by Task Force Delta. He is presently assigned to the staff of the Army War College.

Channon believes First Earth will be an operational battalion within five years, as pressures to counter terrorism and improve the manpower in the army grow. That hope may not be unrealistic, considering the influence of some battalion enthusiasts. Four-star general Robert Shoemaker, the army's deputy chief of staff for personnel, calls Channon "the army's leading futurist" and sees the First Earth Battalion and the warrior monk as a model for the future.

Task Force Delta is definitely an official organization. Members communicate via the army computer network. "Deltanet," the official designator of the U.S. Army Delta Force Computer Conference and Electronic Mail Network, has over a thousand members, who call themselves "the tribe."

Naturally, "the tribe" does not command universal acclaim, even within the army.

The lack of a consensus is a personal matter to Channon, who has been accused by colleagues of "spending too much time in California." Channon comes from a military family. His father graduated from West Point; Channon got an appointment but flunked the English exam for admission. He majored in "art and ROTC" (reserve officer training) at the University of Kentucky. After a tour in Germany, Channon returned to the United States, married and bought a home, and then went to Vietnam. Five months later, he was the only platoon leader in the battalion left alive: "I realized how precious life is after I was almost killed three times on the same day. Basically, I woke up!"

In Vietnam, he put his art training to work, devising a graphics map grid for pig castrators and wood carriers, who regularly crossed the border and pinpointed enemy strongpoints.

After his combat tour, Channon returned for graduate work at the University of Kentucky. There his paintings of the war won the Students for a Democratic Society's (SDS) "Green Commode Award" because there was no blood. Today his paintings hang in five museums. Channon's drawings illustrate the First Earth Battalion's "Soft Tactics Manual."

Channon studied television journalism and systems analysis, convinced that new technologies had changed traditional warfare forever. "We relied on smart bombs instead of smart soldiers, and that's why we lost Vietnam," Channon says with conviction. "Firepower doesn't win wars."

Firepower is the weakest link in the hierarchy of force, according to the "Soft Tactics Manual." Stronger than firepower is the force of will, stronger still is spirit, and love is the strongest force of all.

"Will is strictly staying power. North Vietnam used will to win. Their concept of war is forever," according to Channon.

"Spirit is the open manifestation of how the whole nation feels," and it is television, Channon feels, that has made spirit decisive. "When Samoza's soldiers shot that newsman on TV, countries turned their back on him within a day. At that moment in history, might no longer made right."

The early Iranian revolution was another demonstration of spirit—a million Iranians chanting and dancing in the streets and on the television networks. The United States, Channon says, should have countered with the ultimate force, love.

"We needed to demonstrate to the Iranians that we thought we were right, but that they were right too, that we accept them with open arms and ask them to accept us." Unfortunately, according to Channon, neither country had reached a level of consciousness where acceptance was feasible.

Channon's ideal warrior monk would be proficient at every level of force. At the monastery, the plan of the day will begin with yoga stretching. A primal scream, "to feel their power," will replace the traditional military bugle reveille. The monks will breakfast on Belgian waffles, protein sponges that digest for hours, ginseng tea for emotional balance, and amphetamines for pep.

When it's operational, Channon plans peacetime work for the First Earth Battalion. Warrior monks will clear landing sites for UFOs and prepare to communicate with the ETs. Deserts in the American West will be irrigated by canals from Canada, and the battalion will harvest kudzu (a Japanese vine used to make hay, grain alcohol, and methane) in the Southeast to make the army energy self-sufficient.

Training will consist of headwork, bodywork, spiritwork, biowork, and psiwork, symbolized by a man with his head, arms and legs stretched out into a five-pointed star.

Headwork consists of consciousness raising to solve life's problems. Bodywork includes muscular development, breath yoga, and the martial arts. Spiritwork means people learning to grow together. Biowork utilizes the earth's energy. Psiwork develops and applies parapsychology.

At the "high-tech test bed" where Channon was assigned, the army is already experimenting with one of the New Age bodywork concepts Channon recommended: the Dallas Cowboys' physical training system. In addition to rigorous conditioning, Dallas floats football players in a sensory deprivation tank to develop their concentration. The tank's water is at body temperature, and all outside sound and light are kept out. Players are supposed to think about football, but suffer from hallucinations if they stay in too long. Soldiers would think about fighting instead of football.

Fighting monks endeavor to restrain or win over the enemy, not kill him. Channon prefers to teach aikido, which emphasizes turning the opponent's force against him, rather than more lethal martial arts like karate and kung fu, which emphasize blows. "The objective of martial arts training is spiritual development. The physical part is simply to deliver yourself from a fear state. Then you're able to approach people openly, trustingly, knowing your body will react instinctively to defend you if need be." Aikido also fosters love. "People with guns don't approach others lovingly. An aikido master would."

Psiwork relies on diet and meditation. "At present we recommend that the soldier eat only nuts, seeds, fruit, and vegetables to clean out the system and increase psychic awareness. Occasional meat keeps the body's antitoxins in working order."

The First Earth Battalion will organize itself informally: uniforms without uniformity, structure without status, and unity powered by diversity. Battalion members will be multiracial, each race contributing to "rainbow power." "Each race has all these attributes, of course," says Channon, "but I think blacks could offer the most soul; browns, heart; reds, grace; whites, vision; and yellows, balance."

Women will fight beside men. "No one has the right to tell any American she can't fight for her country," says Channon, and besides, women are "great at intelligence projections. Cultural conditioning has left their intuition better developed, so they're better at sensing where the enemy is."

Battalion combat doctrine relies on "psyching up" the troops with amphetamines and music, possibly at the cost of making it easy for the enemy to know where the warrior monks are. Inside New Age tanks, headphones (not needed for radio communications, because warrior monks use ESP) will play "something like the sound of a one-hundred-ten-piece black high school band when they are really jiving, and the crescendos keep getting higher and higher." Outside speakers will blare hard rock out of sync: "Can't you see some kid from the Ukraine listening to fifty tanks rolling down the valley at night blasting out Black Sabbath?"

That idea isn't so new. The army tried to scare Chinese peasants during the Korean War by painting tigers on the front of tanks. The garish teeth had an effect, according to captured Chinese antitank gunners: "Very good to sight guns on."

Modern combat doctrine, in fact, emphasizes concealment,

because the new smart weapons are so deadly once a target is pinpointed. Nevertheless, the army ordered Channon to design a whole motorcade of New Age armor, including a Honda motorcycle with lasers on the handlebars and a mortar on the rear fender, and a dune buggy with gatling guns on the rollbars.

Channon thinks New Age armor will help morale. "The kids already know how to drive dune buggies, and they like the big tires," he explains.

The First Earth Battalion will also restore the rituals of war. "The war paint and feathers, the chants and dances, all helped make the Indians such great warriors," says Channon. "The army needs flashier uniforms and war whoops."

Where does consciousness raising end and practical soldiering resume? How serious can the army be about troops levitating across rivers and curing radiation sickness with acupuncture?

Reveille at boot camp does not yet begin with a primal scream, at least not an official scream. I have some doubt that it ever will, but powerful interests do take Channon seriously. Two four-star generals, Shoemaker and Glenn K. Otis, belong to the Delta network, along with six major generals—Sam Wetzel, Dale Vesser, Bob Moore, Jack Merritt, James Ellis, and Bob Elton—three brigadier generals—Allen Omo, Harden Olson, and Rick Brown—the deputy assistant secretary of defense for Equal Opportunity and Safety, Dr. Sharon Lord, and the Dallas Cowboy conditioning coach, Bob Ward.

Membership in and correspondence through the Delta computer network remains mostly unofficial, although the annual Task Force Delta meeting at the Army War College is usually a "command performance"—military slang for a mandatory official function. Delta force concepts have had an effect, particularly in the training commands. The first thing General Shoemaker did after assuming the post of deputy chief of staff for personnel was organize a Task Force Delta conference "to draw up an organizational plan for training leaders" to be presented to the general staff. The report adopted by the conference calls on the army to select "super fighters, soldiers who are calm, swift, deadly." Its master plan is AIRLAND BATTLE 2000 and stresses "research into the functioning and processes of the mind . . . soldiers to program and reprogram their mind and actions into a deadly warrior-fighting capability."

Strange as the First Earth Battalion may seem, it is really a rather traditional American concept, descendant from a long line of self-help organizations.

The American faith in self-help and the self-made man is the faith in the *practical* power of positive religion—spiritual technology, if you will. "Learn to pray correctly, scientifically," writes Norman Vincent Peale, the most popular author of the genre. "Avoid slipshod praying."

Right thinking releases fabulous energies. "There is enough power in *you,*" Peale promises, "to blow the city of New York to rubble. That, and nothing less, is what advanced physics tells us."

Channon computerizes Peale's scientific prayer and implies he would rather blow Moscow to rubble: "If you look for clear examples of where the free world has an advantage over the world of nonbelievers, you will discover *two resources* that clearly stand out in our favor. They are God and microelectronics. The beauty in that is you can use the microelectronics to project the spirit . . . brains work like that. Hence the field of psychoelectronic weaponry."

The American faith in the power of positive thinking is a democratic faith, the faith in the potential of the ordinary man. If anything, that faith actually rejects special talent or genius. The common man rises from rags to riches through the sweat on his brow, not the power of his intellect. Religion, says Norman Vincent Peale, is "a simple, workable technique of thinking and acting" that "emphasizes scientific spiritual principles that have been demonstrated in the laboratory of personal experience."

Again and again, the same theme of the power of the ordinary man and the danger of the intellect appears in parapsychology.

Col. Mike Malone, one of the "tribal elders" of the First Earth Battalion, repeated the theme in his official report on Task Force Delta's 1982 meeting at the Army War College:

> I am one of the tribal elders . . . my name is "The Mullet Man."
> I am known as the one who casts nets. And I try to tell people that of all those who cast nets, most should be concerned with the catching, but some, at least, should focus more on the casting than the catching. I live with, fish for, and push the cause of the mullet, because he is a "low-class" fish. He is simple. He is honest. He moves around in great formations and columns. He does damn near all the work. But he is also *noble*. He is, in many ways, like another noble thing I once loved and worked with called "soldier."

Even Puthoff and Targ subscribe to the faith. Remote viewing, they assert repeatedly, is a power everyone might possess—if they forsake the analytic powers of the human mind for faith in the power of belief.

"In our experience," say Puthoff and Targ, "anyone who decides for himself that it is safe to experience paranormal functioning can learn to do so. In our experiments, we have never found anyone who could not perceive scenes, including buildings, roads, and people, even those at great distances and blocked from ordinary perception."[1]

Those who would achieve the power of faith must reject things of the intellect. "It is essential," say Puthoff and Targ, "to avoid trying to figure it out by analysis."[2]

A number of organizations exist outside established psi research communities, devoted to applied uses of parapsychology. Among the more apparently "lunatic fringe" of these is the United States Psychotronics Association, Inc. (USPA). Psychotronics, basically, is the amplification of psychic energies by electronic devices.

The USPA sells a bewildering variety of psychotronic devices. Most require a "specimen" to work—a lock of hair, a spot of blood on a piece of blotting paper, or a small unmutilated photograph. According to one catalog, "It is important that the specimen not be handled by anyone else because this is a representative piece of you . . . you have a sole radiational type of pattern that is applicable only to your own universe within."

A pocket body polarizer resembles a penlight and sells for twenty-one dollars. A specimen is required. "The object of the pocket body polarizer," according to the catalog, "is to correct the unpolar proportions of radiation due to tiredness, weakness, inability to concentrate, insomnia, coupled with aches or pains otherwise unaccountable. . . . Upon wearing the polarizer these symptoms vanish almost at once." Males wear the polarizer on the left side of the body, females on the right. Immersion in water renders this instrument powerless. An "earth radiation neutralizer" counteracts "negative earth radiation." No specimen is required; the price is fifty dollars. A "psi barrier" protects the owner from psychic attack, negative energy, and psychic control at a price— three hundred and twenty-five dollars.

Despite the whacky sound of these devices, USPA has got some attention from U.S. government agencies. As described earlier, the navy bought a psychotronic "multispectral image analyzer" from Dr. Charles Whitehouse, a chiropractor and USPA board member. The U.S. Air Force considered installing "psi barriers" designed by Robert Beck, another member, in Minuteman missile silos to protect crews from psychic attack.

The best-known USPA member, Lt. Col. Thomas E. Bearden, U.S. Army (retired) himself a retired Pentagon analyst, blames Soviet psychotronic experimentation for sundry lights in the sky, Legionnaire's disease, trace radiation in southern Sweden, the "greatest wave of UFO contactee cases in history," the sinking of the U.S. nuclear submarine *Thresher*, and a mysterious wave of cattle mutilations in the Midwest.

The unsolved mutilation of a young horse in Kansas, according to Bearden, symbolizes that "the youth [the young soldiers] will be emasculated, helpless before the onslaught at first of the first Warsaw Pact hordes and immediately thereafter of the Soviet psychotronic superweapons." Worse fates await us: the horrible "possibility of raising cattle mutilations to the last final step, the paranormal mutilation of the human female."

The Soviets have not caused these atrocities deliberately. Unwittingly, they have aroused mankind's collective unconscious, which Bearden calls ZARG. ZARG could do more than castrate cattle; he has the power "to pull the very stars out of orbit, disrupt the earth or the solar system, stop the earth in its orbit, or even change the fundamental laws of nature itself." Since ZARG is unconscious, it is by definition a "sleeping" giant, which will awake filled with fury should the Soviets ever use the fourth-generation psychotronic weapons Bearden says they have deployed to "denude the strategic capability of the free world with a single shot—the teeth of the U.S. dragon can be extracted by the Soviet psychotronic weapons almost at will."

Bearden published his theories before his retirement, and his papers are available through the Defense Documentation Center.[3] Several officers I contacted recalled that Bearden's fanaticism did more to discredit psychotronics in the Pentagon than help, but supporters remain. Lieutenant Colonel Alexander, for one, takes Bearden's theories seriously. Alexander even delivered a paper to the 1981 USPA national convention in Dayton, Ohio. The army, while careful to note that Alexander's paper represented the views of the author alone and not an official position, sent unsolicited copies to congressional offices. Elizabeth Rauscher, a well-known physicist and occasional consultant to Puthoff and Targ at Stanford Research Institute as well as the Department of Defense, also attended the convention.

However the critics might complain, friends like Alexander and Rauscher have got Bearden access to the Pentagon since his retirement. The Defense Technical Information Center lists a dozen contracts in which Bearden was the chief researcher. The army's Redstone Arsenal's Sam-D Project, which developed the new Patriot ground-to-air antiaircraft missile, funded Bearden studies on the "photonic barrier modulator," the Soviet psychotronic weapon Bearden claims caused Legionnaire's disease; the "hyperspatial nuclear howitzer," which supposedly transmits bombs anywhere in the universe; and an antimissile system based on a polar time warp, which would send Soviet missiles careening into the dinosaur era. The Army Medical Intelligence and Information Command funded separate studies of the hyperspatial howitzer by German researchers. Their report, "Bombs from Hyperspace," is unclassified but restricted to official use only.

Several Bearden contracts deal with his theoretical link among ESP, UFOs, and quantum physics. According to the abstract of a technical report delivered by the Computer Sciences Corporation of Huntsville, Alabama, Bearden

> . . . introduces a speculative model of mind and matter and their interaction that is consistent with the experimental basis of physics, and which offers mechanisms for paranormal phenomena of all types, including UFO phenomena. . . . A solution to the problem of the nature of the mind is generated, using the author's fourth law of logic, and a seven-dimensional hyperspatial physical model of the living biosphere is developed. Using this model, an infinite dimensional cotemporal hyperspatial model of the physical universe complete with all its life forms is constructed. Levels of unconsciousness—including the collective human species unconscious—emerge naturally as types of crosstalk between hyperframes. . . . At the level of collective human species unconscious, the psychokinesis is sufficient to materialize symbolic tulpoids (thought forms), given a sufficient stress stimulus in large groups. Using the cold war as the major stress stimulus on mankind since World War II, the author shows that most major UFO waves in the literature precisely fit the model.*

In a similar report for the Systems Development Corporation, also in Huntsville, Alabama, Bearden solves "the one human problem . . . and its relation to the UFO phenomena."

*Quoted from a classified Department of Defense abstract of Bearden's study.

Some of Bearden's theories have actually been officially adopted at the command level. The 1981 *Fire Support Mission Area Analysis (FSMAA)*, a highly classified periodic document that promulgates official army combat doctrine, noted that psychotronic weapons, which it lumps into "cryptomental" technologies, might affect the stamina and performance of field artillerymen:

> This area attempts to direct attention to the relatively unexplored, unexploited human technologies in such areas as influence, communications, thinking, learning, and stress reduction. Discussions of this area represent an excursion into a largely unknown realm which appears to possess significant military application.

The *FSMAA* explicitly defines psychotronics as "a union between mind and matter—a form of energy about which little is apparently known in the United States, but which appears to have significant military application and implication," including psychotronic "mind-jamming":

> While considering the subject of Psychotronics, it is essential that people remain open-minded and recognize that the technology, physics, and mathematics involved are real, and not matters of the occult or supernatural. Details of Psychotronics offer a "physics of metaphysics"—a fully developed theory of paranormal phenomena that unites physics and psychology. . . .
>
> Supernormal happenings arise from the laws of the mind, and phenomena like extrasensory perception and telepathy are not as out of the ordinary and inexplicable as they are generally considered to be.

The report concludes that the "key deficiency in this area is the apparent absence of an organized U.S. military or government effort to investigate the offensive and defensive potential of psychotronics. This deficiency is especially significant in light of the reported research by the Soviet Union in the area of Psychotronic

Warfare." Lieutenant Colonel Alexander's *Military Review* article on psychic warfare is an appendix to the report.

The warriors of the First Earth Battalion think "something BIG is about to happen." The army stands at the threshold of the New Age, an age of psychotronics, the rise of the common man, and the warrior monk. The tribe of the army leadership is ready to accept the new shamans, new power, new energy.

Of course, not everyone in the army approves, even at the tenth annual tribal gathering of the army leadership. The "flat-planet" soldiers, the elder noted, "couldn't figure out what the hell was goin' on."

NOTES

1. Puthoff and Targ, *Mind Reach,* p. 5.
2. Ibid., p. 103.
3. For example, Bearden, *An Approach to Understanding Psychotronics,* DDC, June 1976, AD-A027866. Bearden published several similar studies, all available through DDC.

7 · UNCERTAIN THOUGHTS

In my proposal to my publisher for this book, I had grandiose plans for this last chapter. I promised a "how-to" guide to detecting frauds and charlatans, the final word on the validity of parapsychological research, and a call for congressional hearings on psychic warfare.

Since then I've decided that Congress has enough to do, and I'm less certain about the other two points.

I am still willing to bet against parapsychology researchers ever proving their case, but not as much as I might have bet when I began writing this book. I no longer object to modest government funding, as long as it's modest. If I'm wrong and the parapsychologists are right, that knowledge might revolutionize science.

As for my "how-to" guide, I've learned my method for detecting frauds and charlatans does not depend so much on my great mind as the seat of my pants. The method, in fact, requires only a sentence—people who agree with me speak the truth, and those who disagree are frauds and charlatans.

I haven't found a better method. An investigative reporter needs an instinctive sense of the truth, or needs to believe himself so gifted, or at least needs to learn to bludgeon contrary voices into silence. I like to think of myself as gifted, although I do know how to bludgeon the opposition.

To some extent, I've learned that people are likely to believe what interests them and disbelieve anything they find boring. When I began this book, the sole attraction was the money.

Psychics bored me, and so I didn't believe in them. They bore me less today, but I'm more likely to be fascinated by the skeptic.

I am not the first to learn this lesson. When Rudyard Kipling visited the United States as a young journalist, he met the equally great American author, Mark Twain. Twain had just finished an article on mathematics, an article he found interesting, although he hardly understood a word. Facts have a certain feel, they interest people, Twain noted. He gave Kipling some apropos advice: "First get the facts—then you can distort them as much as you like."

There is a tendency in the psychic community to distort the facts before getting them straight, sorting out the good experimental results from the discredited experiments and unreliable anecdotes. Parapsychologists often seem to think fancifully about what has been accomplished, and to measure any new experiment against the voluminous, but uncontrolled and scientifically useless anecdotal reports of psychic miracles. Facts get ignored, and even favorable facts sink into the morass of anecdotes. It is a tendency not limited to the psychic community, of course, but the temptation seems especially strong.

Certainly, the record of controlled research to date is sufficient to justify an investment in further research without the endless repetition of dubious anecdotal reports.

I am not convinced the parapsychologists have established beyond a reasonable doubt that there is such a thing as a psychic phenomenon; my own doubts seem quite reasonable to me. I am convinced there is something worth investigating, even if all we finally learn is the psychology of bad experimentation.

My doubts about whether or not parapsychologists should devote a significant portion of their effort to military-related research are considerably more serious—serious to the point where I should now say no.

As I've stated before, my objections have nothing whatsoever to do with a general bias against military research. I served five years in the navy myself.

The military wants quick solutions to practical problems, problems parapsychologists haven't solved. The recent interest in so-called applied psi stems largely from failure in the laboratory.

The failures of psychic warfare projects in military laboratories, the record shows, have often been among the most irresponsible experiments ever reported: the séances with dead Soviet agents, the multispectral image analyzer that supposedly detects submarines with a photo, the hyperspatial nuclear howitzer, and the antimissile time warp over the North Pole, to review only a few.

I am too realistic to believe that anyone is going to turn to government grants, particularly in a community so starved for funds, funds to which that community has a legitimate scientific claim. Nevertheless, it is my firm belief that if for no other reason, the effects of security classifications make it inadvisable for the parapsychologists to engage in military-related research.

If the Scanate report were not classified top secret, we might be able to resolve questions about its validity. The test sounds good, from everything I have learned, but who can be sure? I have no way of verifying how targets were selected, how the results were judged, how the subjects were isolated, or any of a hundred other details that would be found routinely in an unclassified research paper.

On the other hand, if the antimissile time warp and fiascoes of that ilk were unclassified, open to public scrutiny, those researchers and the officials who hired them might get the consideration (I think) they deserve—severance checks.

Perhaps it is the fear of such ridicule that has driven parapsychology research so deeply under the cover of the classification system. In the CIA, according to former White House aide Barbara Honegger, the very word *parapsychology* is classified and can be used only over secure (encrypted) phone lines. Any CIA report mentioning *psi* is automatically classified top secret or higher.

The navy, as we have seen, goes to even greater lengths to

conceal their involvement, although they sponsored the most important research, including Scanate. Even fully cleared congressmen can't penetrate the cover. In March 1980, Congressman Bob Kastenmeier asked the Pentagon whether the department had ever sponsored psychic research at Stanford Research Institute or anywhere else. Judging from Kastenmeier's report to an interested constituent, the response was less than candid, considering that the navy had sponsored that research for the past eight years:

> Regarding Stanford Research Institute's research in parapsychology and/or psychic phenomena, the digging did not produce much here. It is suggested that possible contracts may have gone out from the National Science Foundation, National Institute of Health, the Department of Defense, or the National Academy of Sciences. However, each one queried said that the print-outs of their outside contracts were not specific enough to tell just what the research involved.
>
> A call to the local office of SRI elicited the suggestion that it was probable that such research was classified, and would generally not be open to public inspection.

I personally had only marginally better luck with a computer search of Pentagon records. I obtained the search through the Defense Technical Information Center, which accesses Department of Defense records classified secret, confidential, or unclassified. Top secret records are not carried in the system. The search used the key words *dowsing, extrasensory perception, hyperspace, map dowsing, parapsychology, psychoelectronics, psychokinetics, psychotronics, telekinesis,* and *telepathy.*

About fifty reports turned up, all unclassified. What's interesting is what didn't turn up. None of the SRI contracts are in the system, even the few that were unclassified. None of the intelligence reports on Soviet research, which have been released under the Freedom of Information Act, were listed. Presumably the most interesting reports, like Scanate, are classified top secret and outside the system.

So where do we stand? Is there a psychic cold war? Ingo Swann, one of the stars of Scanate and presumably one of the leading warriors, addressed that question at the 1979 Army Operations Conference:

> Psychic warfare is quite close to the surface in most of us, I have found. I would like to draw your attention to the Force portrayed in *Star Wars*. It is not very well explained in the film, yet everyone I have talked to understands completely what the Force is, and further, accepts the fact that unblemished pure humanitarian psychic abilities are likely to be besieged by those who will seek to use psychic aptitudes to enhance their power, their personal goals of control over all other human beings.*

Swann considers resistance to parapsychology research in the West "the first of the three stages of psychic warfare," part disinformation and part stubbornness. "I am convinced beyond any doubt that the Soviet Union is far, far in advance of the United States in psychic research."

I think Swann is wrong on this point. If we've learned anything about the Soviet research, we've learned its status is as tentative and ambiguous as similar projects here.

The second stage of the present psychic cold war, according to Swann, is "the many forms of external manipulations that are known to change the interior psychic formation of any man or woman . . . the most gross of these techniques was the early form of brainwashing, where subtle suggestion was enforced and embedded along with vicious and violent physical trauma. Since that time, however, we now have the refined techniques known as subliminal persuasion behavior modification and various forms of covert mind control."

Swann probably understates the second point. I have said little of these techniques, in part because many are electronic and not "psychic" in the generally understood sense, in part because little

*Proceedings of the U.S. Army Operations Conference, 1979.

information is available, and in part for another reason—security.

There is, according to the best sources, a real threat in the electronic manipulation of the human mind. The possibility arose from research that attempted to explain telepathy electromagnetically. Unfortunately, although the researchers did not discover, as they sought, that thoughts could influence long-range electromagnetic radiation, they did discover that long-range electromagnetic radiation might influence the mind.

According to Barbara Honegger, "the fundamental reason for the increased interest" in psychic warfare, and the area where the Pentagon spends most of its estimated six-million-dollar annual budget for psychic or related research, "is initial results coming out of laboratories in the United States and Canada that certain amplitude and frequency combinations of external electromagnetic radiation in the brain-wave frequency range are capable of bypassing the external sensory mechanism of organisms, including humans, and directly stimulating higher-level neuronal structures in the brain. This electronic stimulation is known to produce mental changes at a distance, including hallucinations in various sensory modalities, particularly auditory."

According to Langley-Porter's Alan Gevins, who is generally cautious and skeptical of psychic claims, the reality may be worse. Extremely low frequency radiation (ELF), which the navy has proposed as a submarine communication system because the thousand-mile long wave forms are unobstructed by water, might be capable of shutting off the brain, killing everyone in 10 thousand square miles or larger target area. "No one paid any attention to the biological affects of ELF for years," says Gevins, "because the power levels are so low. Then we realized that because the power levels are so low, the brain could mistake the outside signal for its own, mimic it [a process known as bioelectric entrainment], and respond when it changes."

It is possible the Soviets have actually tested this technique. The microwaves beamed at the U.S. embassy in Moscow might have been a test. The navy is still investigating an even more ominous possibility—a rash of aircraft carrier crashes in 1980 and 1981 might have been caused by electromagnetic waves beamed at incoming pilots from the Soviet spy ships that shadow the U.S. fleet. Even a tiny uncertainty, electronically induced at that last critical second before an aircraft touches down on the pitching deck of a carrier, might cause disaster.

I must stress that these results and speculations are tentative. There is no reason for panic, and the United States has invested adequate resources to investigation of the problem. There is no need for a psychic Manhattan Project.

The third phase of psychic warfare, according to Ingo Swann, is the actual use of psychics in espionage or war. I don't spend sleepless nights worrying about that prospect myself.

I am more concerned that the rising interest in parapsychology will divert public attention from more conventional research that has less to promise but, so far at least, more to offer. I am disturbed when a five hundred-page congressional report on future research devotes three pages to parapsychology and not a word to conventional brain research such as that at Langley-Porter.

I also do not wish to hear from any more crackpots who claim the CIA assassinated their cat with psychic bullets. The final word, from President John F. Kennedy, I dedicate to them.

During the Cuban missile crisis of 1961, a Department of Defense communications expert consulted the resident CIA psychics and brought their dire predictions to the attention of Robert Kennedy. The Soviets would not yield to a blockade, they said. The president should order a "surgical" strike by air force planes against the Soviet missiles.

Robert reportedly took the psychic intelligence to his brother with mock seriousness.

"Don't sweat it," said the president.

If I'd never heard of bioelectric entrainment, I'd say that was still good advice.

BIBLIOGRAPHY

For those interested in detailed research, I include the following bibliography compiled by Marcello Truzzi:

For those who want to do further reading, three books are essential:

Ebon, Martin; *Psychic Warfare: Threat or Illusion?*, N.Y.: McGraw-Hill, 1983. Concentrates on the Soviet side, based on extensive documentation and interviews with Soviet emigres.

Puthoff, Harold and Russell Targ; *Mind Reach: Scientists Look at Psychic Ability*, N.Y.: Delta, 1978. Puthoff and Targ's own account of the Scanate experiments.

Wilhelm, John; *The Search for Superman*, N.Y.: Pocket Books, 1976 (out of print). Since writing this book, Wilhelm has begun to doubt the validity of SRI's remote viewing experiments, but this remains the best first-hand account of those tests written by an outsider.

Bibliography of English Language Articles on U.S. Government, Soviet, and Chinese Efforts in Parapsychology *

Adamenko, V.G., "The Accumulation of Bioelectrical Energy," *Psycho-energetic Systems*, 2 (1977), 79–80.

———, "Objects Moved at a Distance by Means of a Combined Bio-electric field," in *Abstracts, Twentieth International Congress of Psychology*. Tokyo: International Congress of Psychology, 1972.

———, "Psi and Psychical Fields," in W.G. Roll (ed.), *Research in Parapsychology, 1978*. Metuchen, N.J.: Scarecrow Press, 1979.

*Compiled by Marcello Truzzi with special thanks to Stanley Krippner, Rhea White, Ron McRae, Martin Gardner, Martin Ebon, and John Wilhelm.

———, "Controlled Movement of Objects," *Journal of Paraphysics,* 6 (1972), 180–226.

Agnew, Irene, "Parapsychology in Russia," *Science Digest,* July 1972, pp. 69–71.

Alexander, John B., "The New Mental Battlefield: 'Beam Me Up, Spock," *Military Review,* December 1980, pp. 47–54.

Anderson, Jack, "Yes, Psychic Warfare Is Part of the Game," *Washington Post,* February 5, 1981.

———, "Pentagon Invades Buck Rogers' Turf," *Washington Post,* June 8, 1981.

"Another Case of 'Eye-less vision' reported in Soviet Newspaper," *International Journal of Parapsychology,* 6 (Winter 1964), p. 23.

A.R.E. Journal (Association for Research and Enlightenment), March 1972.

Arnold, Sidney, "Seances in Soviet Russia," *London Forum,* April 1935, pp. 255–257.

Asher, Jules, "Soviet Psychologists Reverse Stand, Urge New Action on Psychic Research, *APA Monitor* (American Psychological Association), *5,* 4 (April 1974), 1 & 8.

Bakirov, A.G., "The Geological Possibilities of Biophysical Method," *Proceedings, First International Conference on Psychotronic Research.* Prague: Cerven, 1973.

Banarjee, H.N., "Parapsychology in Russia," *Indian Journal of Parapsychology,* 3 (1961–62), 43–51.

Bannister, et al., "U.S. Defense Dept. Documents Warn of Threat from Russian Psychic Experiments," *National Enquirer,* p. 37.

Bashkirov, G., "The little girl 'sensation,'" *International Journal of Parapsychology,* 7 (August 1965), 379–394.

———, "Not fantasy, not mysticism, not hypnosis," *International Journal of Parapsychology,* 7 (August 1965), 402–407.

Bearden, Tom, *Excalibur Briefing.* San Francisco: Strawberry Hill Press/ Walnut Hill Books, 1980.

———, "Soviet Psychotronic Weapons: A Condensed Background," *Specula,* March–June, 1978.

Bechterev, W., "Direct Influence of a Person Upon the Behavior of Animals," *Journal of Parapsychology,* 13 (September 1949), 166–176.

Beck, R.C., "Extreme Low Frequency Magnetic Fields Entrainment: A Psychotronic Warfare Possibility?" *Association for Humanistic Psychology Newsletter,* April 1978.

Beloff, John, "ESP and Soviet Skepticism," *New Scientist, 41* (January 9, 1969), 88–89. (Letter)

Bird, Christopher, *The Divining Hand.* N.Y.: Dutton, 1979. pp. 229–245.

Bonch-Burevich, B., "Can One Read Thoughts?" *International Journal of Parapsychology, 7* (August 1965), 395–398.

Borzymowski, Andrzei, "Parapsychology in Poland," *International Journal of Parapsychology, 4* 4 (1962).

Bradna, Jiri, "Interpersonal Relations and Energetic Transfer," *Proceedings, First International Conference on Psychotronic Research.* Prague, Cerven, 1973.

Caldwell, Carol, "Beyond ESP," *New Times,* April 3, 1978, pp. 43–50.

Chamberlain, J., "Soviet 'Ultimate Weapon'?" New Haven *Register,* June 21, 1976.

Chijov, V., "Wonder in a Sleve," *Journal of Paraphysics,* 2 (1968), 109–11. (Translation of article in *Pravda,* June 24, 1968.)

Coates, James, "Psychic Spy Died, No Word Since," *Detroit Free Press* (from Chicago Tribune), August 10, 1977, p. 6–A.

Coffin, Tris, "Brain Rays: Russia's Secret Weapon?" *Coronet, 38* (June 1955), 120–125.

Cohen, Daniel, "ESP: Science or Delusion?" *Nation, 202* (May 9, 1966), 550–552.

Dean, Douglas, "Amazing Russian ESP Tests—I Saw Them with My Own Eyes," *National Enquirer,* Oct. 1, 1972, p. 5.

————, "I Witnessed Startling Advances in Russian ESP Research," *National Enquirer,* Sept. 24, 1972, p. 4.

Defense Intelligence Agency (author's name still classified), *Paraphysics R & D—Warsaw Pact (U).* Washington, D.C.: Defense Intelligence Agency, March 30, 1978. (# DST-1810S-202-78).

de Maigret, Pamela Painter, "PK Training in Russia," *Fate,* May 1976, pp. 36–44.

" 'Dermal Vision' among Children 7 to 12 Years," *International Journal of Parapsychology, 7* (August 1965), 434.

Dick, William, "Russians Perfecting ESP for Spying," *National Enquirer,* January 9, 1972, p. 8.

Dubrov, A.N., "The Interaction of Biological Objects with Time and Space," *Psychoenergetic Systems,* 1 (1976), 209–214.

————, "Biogravitation and Psychotronics," *Impact of Science on Society, 24.* 4 (1974), 31–32.

————, *The Geomagnetic Field and Life: Geomagnetobiology.* N.Y.: Plenum Press, 1978.

Ebon, Martin, "Russia Explores Inner Space," *Tomorrow,* Winter 1962.
————, "Iron Curtain ESP," *Human Behavior,* November 1978.
————, "Moscow's ESP Dilemma," *The Humanist,* September–October 1977, pp. 42–43.
————, ed., *Psychic Discoveries by the Russians.* N.Y.: Signet/NAL, 1971.
————, "Review of The New Soviet Psychic Discoveries," *Zetetic Scholar,* #1 (1978), 137–138.
————, "Moscow: Behind the ESP Enigma." *New Realities,* 1, 2 (1977), 34ff.

Faddeev, E.T., "The Problem of Telepathy," *Indian Journal of Parapsychology,* 3 (1961–62), 220–30.
Fisher, Dan, "Soviets Widely Preoccupied with Occult," *Los Angeles Times,* October 17, 1979.
Fuller, Curtis, "Parapsychology vs. Communist Dogma," *Fate,* June 1962, pp. 53–58.

Gregory, Anita, "Crackdown on Parapsychology," *New Scientist,* February 13, 1975, 397–398.
————, "A Genuine Russian First in Parapsychology," *Fate,* November 1968 pp. 65–71.
————, "Important Russian Telepathy Findings," *Fate,* July 1971, pp. 45–51.
Gris, Henry, and William Dick, *The New Soviet Psychic Discoveries: A First-Hand Report on the Latest Breakthroughs in Russian Parapsychology.* Englewood Cliffs, N.J.: Prentice-Hall, 1978.
Guliaevm, P.I., "Cerebral Electromagnetic Fields," *International Journal of Parapsychology,* 7 (August 1965), 339–401.

Harvalik, Zarboj, "Anatomical Localization of Human Detection of Weak Electromagnetic Radiation. Experiments with Dowsers," *Physiological Chemistry and Physics,* 10 (1978), 525–534.
Herbert, Benson, "ESP and Soviet Skepticism," *New Scientist,* 41 (January 23, 1969), 192. (Letter)
————, "Kulagina Cine Films, Summary," *Journal of Paraphysics,* 4 (1970), 160–164.

————, "Alla Vinogradova: Demonstration in Moscow," *Journal of Paraphysics,* 6 (1972), 191–208.

————, "Spring in Leningrad: Kulagina Revisited," *Parapsychology Review,* 4 (1973), 5–10.

————, "Psychokinesis in the USSR," *Psychoenergetic Systems,* 3 (1979), 103–108.

————, "East European Press Report: 1979," *Parapsychology Review,* 12, 1 (1981), 23–37.

Inyushin, V.M., "Bioplasma: The Fifth State of Matter," in J. White and S. Krippner (eds.,) *Future Science.* Garden City, N.Y.: Doubleday Anchor, 1977, pp. 115–120.

————, "Biological Plasmas of Human and Animal Organisms," in Z. Dejdak, et al. (eds.), *Symposium of Psychotronics.* Downton, Wiltshire, Paraphysical Laboratory, 1971.

Ivanov, Alexander, "ESP in the USSR," *Fact,* No. 2 (March/April 1964), 41–43.

————, "Soviet Experiments in 'Eyeless Vision,'" *International Journal of Parapsychology,* 6, 1 (Winter 1964), 5–23.

"Journalists and Scientists Discuss Kuleshova 'Phenomenon,' " *International Journal of Parapsychology,* 7 (August 1965), 375–378.

Kazninsky, B.B., *Biological Radio Communications.* Springfield, Va.: Clearing house for Federal Scientific and Technological Information, April 1, 1963. (#AD 415.676)

Kaznacheev, V.P., et al., "Distant Intercellular Interactions in a System of Two Tissue Cultures," *Psychoenergetic Systems,* 1 (1976), 141–142.

Keil, H.H.J., and J. Fahler, "A Strong Case for PK Involving Directly Observable Movements of Objects Recorded on Cine Film," in J.D. Morris, W.G. Roll and R.L. Morris (eds.), *Research in Parapsychology,* 1974. Metuchen, N.J.: Scarecrow Press, 1975.

————, et al. "Directly Observable Voluntary PK Effects," *Proceedings of the Society for Psychical Research,* 56 (1976), 197–235.

Khokhlove, Nicolai, "The Relationship of Parapsychology to Communism," J.B. Rhine, Ed., *Parapsychology Today.* N.Y. 1968.

Kholodov, Y.A., *The Effect of Electromagnetic Fields on the Central Nervous System.* Springfield, Va.: Clearinghouse for Federal Scientific and Technical Information, 1967.

Kitaygorodsky, A., "The Fruits of Education," *Journal of Parapsychology*, 29 (1965), 45–50.

Kogan, I.M., "The Information Theory of Telepathy," paper presented at the Symposium entitled "A New Look at Extra-Sensory Perception," University of Southern California, Los Angeles, June 7–8, 1969.

Kolodny, "When Apples Fall," *Journal of Paraphysics*, 5 (1971), 54–62.

Koshchin, A., "Don't Be Afraid of Facts," *Journal of Parapsychology*, 29 (1965), 51–53.

Kozyrev, N.A., *Possibility of Experimental Study of the Properties of Time*. Washington, D.C.: Joint Publications Research Service, U.S. Department of Commerce, 1968.

Krippner, Stanley, *Song of the Siren: A Parapsychological Odyssey*. N.Y.: Harper and Row, 1972.

——, *Human Possibilities*. Garden City, N.Y.: Doubleday Anchor, 1981.

——, "Soviet Parapsychology: Fiction or Reality?" *Psi News: Bulletin of the Parapsychological Association*, 4, 2 (April 1981), 1–27.

——, and Richard Davidson, "Parapsychology in the USSR," *Saturday Review*, March 18, 1972, pp. 56–60.

——, and Richard Davidson, "A Firsthand Look at Psychotronic Generators," in J. White and S. Krippner (eds.). *Future Science*. Garden City, N.Y.: Doubleday Anchor, 1977, pp. 420–430.

——, "The President's Column," *Newsletter, Division of Humanistic Psychology, American Psychological Association Division 23*, 7, 2 (Fall–Winter 1980), 1–2.

——, and Richard Davidson, "Our Parapsychologists Visit the USSR," *Fate*, November 1972, pp. 91–101. (Reprint)

——, and Richard Davidson, "International Report: Soviets Harness Biological Energy," *Fate*, December 1973, pp. 64–74.

——, and J.L. Hickman, "West Meets East: A Parapsychological Detente," *Psychic*, June 1974.

——, and Richard Davidson, and Nancy Peterson, "Psi Phenomena in Moscow," *Journal of Contemporary Psychotherapy*, 6 (1973), 79–88.

——, and D. Rubin (eds.), *The Kirlian Aura*. Garden City, N.Y.: Doubleday Anchor, 1974.

Kulagin, V.V., "Nina S. Kulagina," *Journal of Paraphysics*, 5 (1971), 54–62.

LaMothe, John D., *Controlled Offensive Behavior—USSR (Unclassified)*. Washington, D.C.: Defense Intelligence Agency, 1972. (#ST-CS-01-169-72)

Lepkowsky, Wil, "Psychic Phenomena: A New Field of Scientific Enquiry?" *Science Forum: A Canadian Journal of Science and Technology*, April 1974.

Lewis, Flora, "Emigre Tells of Research in Soviet in Parapsychology for Military Use," *The New York Times*, June 19, 1977, pp. 1 & 20.

Maire, Louis F., and J.D. LaMothe, *Soviet and Czechoslovakian Parapsychology Research* (Unclassified). Washington, D.C.: Defense Intelligence Agency, 1975. (#DST-1810S-387-75).

Mashkova, V., "Sharpsighted Fingers," *International Journal of Parapsychology*, 7 (August 1965), 368–370.

McConnell, Robert, "Parapsychology in the USSR," *Journal of Parapsychology*, 39 (1975), 129–134.

McGraw, Walter, "Behind the Iron Curtain," *Fate*, March 1964, pp. 27–35.

(McRae, Ron), "Skeptical Eye: Paranormal Pentagon," *Discover*, March 1981, p. 16.

Michrowski, Andrew, "Covert ELF (Extremely-Low-Frequency) Warfare," *Specula*, January–March 1980.

Mitlin, V., "Visit to a Sorcerer," *International Journal of Parapsychology*, 7 (August 1965), 414–417.

Moss, Thelma, "Searching for Psi from Prague to Lower Siberia," *Psychic*, June 1971.

———, "Psychic Research in the Soviet Union," in John White (ed.,), *Psychic Exploration: A Challenge to Science*. N.Y.: G.P. Putnam's Sons, 1974, pp. 469–486.

———, *The Body Electric*. Los Angeles: J.P. Tarcher, 1980, pp. 57–75.

Mutschall, V., "The Present Status of Research in Telepathy in the Soviet Union," *Foreign Science Bulletin*, 4, 8 (1968).

Naumov, E.K., and I.V. Vilenskaya, *Bibliographies on Parapsychology (Psychoenergetics) and Related Subjects—USSR*. Springfield, Va.: National Technical Information Service, March 28, 1972. (#JPSR 5557)

———, (trans. by Ian Stevenson and Emily Williams), *Bibliography of Parapsychology (Psychotronics, Psychoenergetics, and Psychobiophy-*

sics) and Related Problems. Alexandria, Va.: Parapsychological Association, 1981.

NBC Magazine with David Brinkley, Transcript of broadcast of March 13, 1981. N.Y.: National Broadcasting Company. 1981.

"News," Journal of Parapsychology, 38 (1974), 122–128.

Novomeiskii, A.S., "The Nature of the Dermo-Optic Sense," International Journal of Parapsychology, 7 (August 19–5), 341–367.

Ostrander, Sheila, and Lynn Schroeder, Psychic Discoveries Behind the Iron Curtain. Englewood Cliffs, N.J.: Prentice Hall, 1970.

———, "Psychic Enigmas and Energies in the USSR," Psychic, 11 (May–June 1971).

———, eds., The ESP Papers: Scientists Speak Out from Behind the Iron Curtain. N.Y.: Bantam Books, 1976.

———, "Russian Telepath: Wolf Grigorevich Messing," Fate, May 1969, pp. 62–67.

"Parapsychology and Materialism," Journal of Parapsychology, 12 (September 1949), 208–211.

"Parapsychology in the Russian Press," Journal of Parapsychology, 29 (March 1965), 45–53.

Parloff, Morris B., "Superpowers and the Head-Space Race," Psychology Today. 12 (March 1979), 112–114+. (Book review of Superlearning.)

Patrovsky, V., "Magnetized Water and Plant Growth," Proceedings, First International Congress on Psychotronic Research. Prague: Cerven, 1973.

Pratt, J.G., "Glimpses of the Psi Utopia? Reflections Upon an Amazing Account of a Journey through Russia, Bulgaria, and Czechoslovakia," Journal of the American Society for Psychical Research, 65, 1 (1971), 880102.

———, "Extrasensory Perception Research in Russia and Czechoslovakia," International Journal of Neuropsychiatry, September October 1966, 378–385.

———, "Soviet Research in Parapsychology," in B.B. Wolman, ed., Handbook for Parapsychology. N.Y.: Van Mostrand Reinhold, 1977, pp. 883–890

Pratt, J.G., and H.H.J. Keil, "Firsthand Observations of Nina S. Kulagina Suggestive of PK Upon Static Objects," Journal of the American Society for Psychical Research, 67 (1973), 381–390.

"Psychotronics and the Integration of Man," Journal of the American

Society of Psychosomatic Dentistry and Medicine, 23, 3 (1976), 83–89.

Psychic, 2, 6 (June 1971).

Puharich, Andrija; *Uri: A Journal of the Mystery of Uri Geller,* N.Y. Doubleday, 1975.

Puharich, Henry K., "Can Telepathy Penetrate the Iron Curtain?" *Tomorrow,* 5, 2 (Winter 1957), 7–16.

Pushkin, V.N., and A.P. Dubrov, *Parapsychology and the New Natural Sciences.* N.Y.: Plenum Press.

Regelson, L., "An Appeal to Soviet and Foreign Public Opinion," *Journal of the Society for Psychical Research, 47* (1974), 521–524.

Rejdak, A., "Telekinesis or Fraud?" *Journal of Paraphysics, 2* (1968), 68–70.

———, "The Kulagina Cine Films: Introductory Notes," *Journal of Paraphysics, 3* (1969), 64–67.

———, "What is Psychotronics?" *Journal of Paraphysics, 8* (1974), 26–29.

Renesberger, Boyce, "Gains in ESP Studies by Soviet Doubted by American Specialists," *The New York Times,* June 19, 1977, p. 20.

Roschin, A., "Don't Be Afraid of Facts," *Journal of Parapsychology, 29* (March 1965), 51–53.

Rossman, M., *New Age Blues.* N.Y.: Dutton, 1979.

"Russians Investigate Fingertip Vision," *Fate,* May 1964, pp. 46–58. (Reprinted from *Soviet Life Today.*)

Ryzl, Milan, "Book Review of Biological Radio," *Journal of Parapsychology,* 26 (September 1962), 221–226.

———, "Book Review of Long-distance Telepathy," *Journal of Parapsychology, 27* (March 1963), 50–55.

———, "Book Review of Mysterious Phenomena of the Human Psyche," *Journal of Parapsychology, 28* (March 1964), 56–59.

———, "Research on Telepathy in Soviet Russia" *Journal of Parapsychology, 25* (June 1961), 75–85.

———, "Parapsychology in Communist Countries of Europe," *International Journal of Parapsychology, 10,* 3 (1968).

———, "ESP in Eastern Europe and Russia," *Psychic, 1,* 1 & 2 (1969).

———, "Review of Biological Radio," *Journal of Parapsychology, 35,* 2 (1971).

———, "Research on Telepathy in the Soviet Union," *Fate,* May 1962, pp. 75–84. (Reprinted)

Schäfer, George, "In Defiance of the Ideologists: Parapsychology in the Soviet Union," *Journal of Parapsychology*, *30* (March 1966), 48–52.

Sedlak, W., "The Electromagnetic Nature of Life," *Proceedings, Second International Congress on Psychotronic Research*. Paris: Institut Metaphysique International, 1975.

Sergeyev, G.A., "KNS Phenomena," *Journal of Paraphysics*, *5* (1971), 47–50.

———, and V.V. Kulagin, "Psychokinetic Effects of Bioplasmic Energy," *Journal of Paraphysics*, 6 (1972), 18–19.

———, G.D. Shushkev, and E.G. Gryanckhin, "The Piezoelectric Detector of Bioplasm," *Journal of Paraphysics*, 6 (1972), 16–18.

She, Zheng, "Parapsychology, Is It Real?" *China Reconstructs*, January 1981, pp. 50–51.

Shpolyanskaya, A.M., et al., "Differences in Biochemiluminescence Intensity of Blood Serum in Tuberculosis and Lung Cancer," *Psychoenergetic Systems*, *1* (1976), 203–204.

"Soviet Psychic Secrets," *San Francisco Chronicle*, June 16, 1977.

Stuckey, William K., "Psychic Power: The Next Superweapon?" *New York Magazine*, December 27, 1976, 47–55.

Techter, David, "ESP Research in Russia," *Fate*, June 1964, pp. 50–56.

Teodorovich, Nadezhada, "Soviet Studies of Parapsychic Phenomena," *Bulletin, Institute for the Study of the USSR*, No. 10, October 1967, pp. 16–28.

———, "Soviet Studies of Parapsychic Phenomena," *Review of Soviet Medical Sciences*, *4*, 1 (1967).

"The Czech Conference on Psychotronics," *Journal of Paraphysics*, *3*, 1/2 (1971).

Thouless, R.H., "Book Review of ESP Research Today," *Journal of Parapsychology*, *38* (March 1974), 85.

———, "Book Review of *Experiments in Mental Suggestion*," *Journal of Parapsychology*, *28* (June 1964), 138–140.

Tiller, W.A., "The Psychokinetic Phenomena of Alla Vinogradova," *Journal of Paraphysics*, 6 (1972), 77–81.

Toth, Robert C., "Times Correspondent in Russia 'Detained' by KGB," *Los Angeles Times*, June 12, 1977, Part I, pp. 6 & 7.

Trisvyatskaya, Valeria, "She 'Sees' with Her Fingers," *Fate*, July 1963, pp. 26–34.

Tserkover, E., "The Talents of Tophic Dadashev," *International Journal of Paraphysics*, *13* (1979), 56–58.

Ullman, M. "Fragments of a Parapsychological Journey," *Newsletter, American Society for Psychical Research,* October 1971.

————, "PK in the Soviet Union," in W.G. Roll, R.L. Morris, and J.D. Morris (eds.), *Research in Parapsychology,* 1973. Metuchen, N.J.: Scarecrow Press, 1974.

Van de Castle, Robert L., "Book Review of *Psychic Discoveries Behind the Iron Curtain,*" *Journal of Parapsychology, 34* (December 1970), 296–299.

Van Hasselt, P., W. Van Immerseel, and J.A.J. Klijn, "Kirlian Photography: The Myth of Bioplasma," *Medikon,* April 1974.

Vardy, A., "Parapsychology versus Marxism-Leninism," *Review of Soviet Medical Science, 3,* 2 (1966), 59–62.

Vasiliev, L.L., *Experiments in Distant Influence:* N.Y.: Dutton, 1962 & 1976.

————, *Mysterious Phenomena of the Human Psyche.* Springfield, Va.: Clearinghouse for Federal Scientific and Technological Information, March 10, 1967. (#AD 661 891)

————, *Experiments in Mental Suggestion.* Church Crookham, Hampshire, England: Institute for the Study of Mental Images, 1963.

————, *Studies in Mental Telepathy.* N.Y.: CCM Corp., 1971.

————, *Mysterious Phenomena of the Human Psyche.* New Hyde Park, N.Y.: University Books, 1965.

Velinov, I., "Recent Soviet Experiments in Telepathy," *Foreign Science Bulletin, 4,* 8 (1968), 13.

"Views on 'Eye-less Vision,' and International Symposium," *International Journal of Parapsychology, 7* (August 1965), 435–448.

Vilenskaya, L.V., "A Scientific Approach to Some Aspects of Psychic Healing," *International Journal of Paraphysics, 10* (1976), 74–78.

Wilhelm, John L., "Psychic Spying?" *Outlook/Washington Post Sunday Magazine,* August 7, 1977, pp. B1 & B5.

Wilkins, Alexander, "Telepathy in Old Tashkent," *International Journal of Parapsychology, 7* (August 1965), 429–434.

Williamson, Tom, "Dowsing Achieves New Credence," *New Scientist, 81* (February 8, 1979), 371–378.

Wolkowski, A.W., W. Sedlak, and J. Zion, "The Utility of Bioelectronics and the Bioplasma Concept in the Study of the Biological Terrain and Its Equilibrium," *International Journal of Paraphysics, 12* (1978), 51–62.

Wortz, E.C., et al., *Novel Biophysical Information Transfer Mechanism.* Torrance, Cal.: Airsearch Manufacturing Company of California, January 14, 1976.

———, A.S. Bauer, R.F. Blackwelder, J.W. Eerkens and A.J. Saur, "An Investigation of Soviety Psychical Research," in Charles T. Tart, H.E. Puthoff, and R. Targ, eds., *Mind at Large: Institute of Electrical and Electronic Engineers Symposia on the Nature of Extrasensory Perception.* N.Y.: Praeger, 1979, pp. 235–260.

Zielinski, Ludmilla, "The Woman Who Could Read Unopened Letters," in Martin Ebon, ed., *The Psychic Reader.* N.Y.: World Publishing Co., 1969. Chapter 1, pp. 3–10.

Zinchenko, V.P., et al., "Parapsychology: Fiction or Fact?" *Soviet Psychology, 12* (Spring 1974), 3–20.

———, and A.N. Leontiev, "Parapsychology," *Great Soviet Encyclopedia,* N.Y.: Macmillan 1978. (Translation of the 1974 edition.)

———, A.N. Leonfiev, B.F. Lomov, and A.R. Luria, "Parapsychology: Fiction or Reality?" in S. Krippner, ed., *Psychoenergetic Systems.* N.Y.: Gordon & Breach, 1979. (Translation of the 1973 article in *Questions of Philosophy.*) Also available as "Parapsychology in the Soviet Union," in Martin Ebon, ed., *The Signet Handbook of Parapsychology.* N.Y.: New American Library/Signet, 1978, pp. 452–465.

Index

Orne, Martin T., 13
Ostrander, Sheila, 33–34, 45
Owen, Dr. A.R., 83–84

paranoia inducer, 48
parapsychology, 3, 22, 26–27, 68
    Nazi, 40–42
Parapsychology Assn., 21, 37–38,
    61
paraphysics, 62
Pease, Marshall, 100
Pentagon, 15, 16, 19, 33–34, 40,
    63, 68–69
Pepper, Claude, 49
Petukhov, Valery, 74–75
Philadelphia experiments, 43
Phillips, Peter R., 35, 36–38
photonic barrier modulation, 53
plants, mind-reading, 13–14, 68
police, use of psychics, 8–14, 63
poltergeists, 28
Pratt, Dr. J. Gaither, 3
precognition, 23
Price, Pat, 100–1, 104, 111–13
Princeton University, 22
Project Scanate, 92–113
psi, 27
psi particle, 73
Psychic Criminology (Hubbard and
    Worring), 10
*Psychic Discoveries Behind the
    Iron Curtain* (Ostrander),
    33–34, 49–50, 73
psychic energy, 73
psychic phenomena, public
    acceptance, 23
psychic research. *See* funding

psychic warfare, 15, 47–69
psychics, in criminal investigations,
    8–14, 63
psychokinesis, 27, 54
Psychophysical Research Lab, 57
psychotronic devices, 125, 129–30
Puharich, Andrija, 79, 80
Puthoff, Harold, 5, 22, 29, 80–84,
    92–113

radioactivity, 57
radiation, 72, 73
Randi, James, 37, 53, 58, 82, 84,
    86, 90
random-number generators, 58
random-number trials, 60
Reagan administration, 17
REM sleep, 2
remote psychological monitors, 78
remote spontaneous psychokinetic
    phenomena (RSPK), 28
remote viewing, 29–30, 48, 54,
    97–102, 113
Reynolds, Craig, 39–40
Robbins, Shawn, 2–3, 56
Robertson, Ron, 53
Roman Catholic Church, 26
Rose, Rep. Charles, 47–49, 107
RSPK, 28

Sagan, Carl, 29, 34
San Jose Search and Rescue Team,
    10
satellite deployed dowsing rod, 17
Schmidt, Helmut, 37
Schroeder, Lynn, 49